# Come And Live

### A Guide For Finding,
### And Living In, Spiritual Reality

By
## Tom C. McKenney

Words For Living Ministries, Inc., Publisher
Marion, KY 42064

first printing Oct. 1981
second printing April 1982
third printing (Hardcover) Oct. 1982
fourth printing June 1986
fifth printing April 2000

Library of Congress Catalog Card Number 84-242781
ISBN 0-934527-00-8

Printed in the United States of America
by
Harris Press
Nashville, Tennessee

## Dedication

To the Lord Jesus Christ, who was dead and is alive forevermore; and to the multitudes of seekers — dead, sick or empty in one way or another — to whom He is saying "Come and Live".

## Acknowledgements

My humble thanks to all who have helped with encouragement, advice and support, especially my family, which has lived out the contents of this book. Special thanks to Ouida Tanner and Kay Towery, through whom the Lord spoke to me about writing, and to my wife Marty and daughter Melissa for wise counsel and much labor.

Illustrations and design by Joe McCormick, Jackson, Tennessee, who has been much more than an artist.

◦◦◦◦◦

All scripture quotations are from the King James Version of the Bible. Amplification, in parentheses, is that of the author, as is underlining for emphasis.

◦◦◦◦◦

## About the Author

Tom Chase McKenney is a graduate of the University of Kentucky and the University of North Carolina. He was an infantry officer and parachutist in the U.S. Marine Corps, serving in Korea and Vietnam. Retired for disability in 1971, he now travels worldwide as a Bible teacher, evangelist and missionary with emphasis on application of the scriptures to everyday living. He is married, the father of four and grandfather of thirteen.

# Foreword

God's people are being destroyed. Some are being destroyed as martyrs, some are being destroyed in accidents, and others by sin, sickness and deception. The vast majority, however, are being destroyed simply by lack of knowledge (Hosea 4:6). I believe God has called me to come against this lack of knowledge. May this book be His instrument for sharing the knowledge which will help to redeem precious lives from destruction, and turn them instead to life, victory and fruitful service in His kingdom.

Tom C. McKenney
Gulfport, Mississippi
January 1981

# Introduction

Every day people are failing — even God's people — failing to live up to their own aspirations (or others' expectations), falling short of goals, falling victim to discouragement, temptations, fears, unable even to "cope" with life, to say nothing of achieving victory in it. Housewives hang up their aprons and walk away, unable to face another day of life as they know it (according to one study, more wives left home in one recent year than did teenagers). Children run from pressures they can no longer face. Priests leave the priesthood, ministers leave the ministry, discouraged, disillusioned and defeated. Missionaries leave the mission field, broken in health and spirit, with little fruit to look back upon. Church membership and attendance steadily decline; the doors of many churches close permanently each day.

Yet our heads spin with a constant barrage of remedies: motivational research, positive thinking, mental science, meditation, oriental mysticism, programs, psychotherapy, occult philosophy, more education, and a great many more. But things don't seem to get better; in fact they get steadily worse.

Suicide — that ultimate expression of hopelessness — is on the increase, with the average age going rapidly down: people are deciding at earlier and earlier ages that there is no hope — many now taking their own lives before the age of 12. And the group that is supposed to have the answers, those in the psychotherapeutic professions, are among the leaders in frequency of emotional breakdowns and suicides.

Is there no hope? Is there no way out of this downward spiral into frustration, failure, despair and destruction?

Yes! There is good news — that's what "gospel" means. God has provided the missing ingredient, and it is not to be found in the power of the mind, or the power of the will, or the power of positive thinking. It is to be found in the life-giving, life-changing, liberating, enabling power of the Spirit of the living God.

And it is for you.

## Table of Contents

# Chapter 1
# Come And Live

"Why will ye die, Oh House of Israel? . . .
turn yourselves and live ye"

(Ezek. 18:31,32)

In north Florida a middle-aged priest
named Frank paces through his large, silent
house in the middle of the night. He comes

from the "right" family, has been educated in the "right" prep schools, universities and seminaries. He is steeped in knowledge of human behavior, history, philosophy and religion. He is supposed to be the man with the answers. Yet he staggers through the stillness of the night drunk, hands uplifted in the air, crying out of the desperate emptiness of his heart, "Yahweh, the Holy One of Israel . . . . where are you?"

In New Orleans, a young Christian man picks up an Indian girl from the streets; her name is Isabel. She is strung out on drugs, high, dirty, her clothes are filthy. She is burned out already, an unwanted bit of society's refuse, although she is only twenty-three. The young man puts her in his car and hurries to New Life for Girls in Pass Christian, Mississippi where she curses David, the local director, and Demi Rodriquez, the national director, with hatred punctuated by filthy words. They just share the love of Jesus with her, and show her that they care. Finally the faint light of hope begins to dawn in the awful darkness of her mind. For a moment she ceases cursing them, looks up through dirty hair and asks, hesitantly, "Can you help me?"

Poles apart, these two, except where it really matters. They are both dying inside, dead in their spirits, going under in a one-sided struggle against hopelessness and the empty darkness of approaching destruction.

Yet there is life to be had, "and that more abundant." There is for Frank and Isabel — and for you — life, freedom, fulfillment, meaning. And this abundant life is within reach — no matter what you have done. Some of us have been robbed of this life by our humanistic education; others have never heard. Some have come to the awful point of hopelessness by way of the classroom and the contemporary church; some got there by way of the suburbs; some by way of disillusionment on the battlefield or in the marketplace. Others arrived by way of the jungle in the streets. But no matter where you started, no matter which path you took, the destination is the same: darkness, despair and death. For truly "There is a way which seemeth right unto a man, but the end thereof are the ways of death" (Prov. 14:12).

Yes — we may all be on different paths, we may all have come from different beginnings, but without the reality of God in our lives the end is the way of death.

Yet God's desire for you isn't death, it is life. And this life is not "just making it," it is rich and abundant. This life is only to be found in God Himself; and Jesus said that we cannot know the Heavenly Father except we first know Him ("I am the Way, the Truth, and the Life; no man cometh unto the Father but by

Me." Jn. 14:6). Jesus also said, "The thief (Satan) cometh not, but for to steal, and to kill, and to destroy: (but) I am come that they might have life, and that they might have it more abundantly" (Jn. 10:10). He really does have life for you — abundant life. He doesn't want you to die; He doesn't want you just to survive; and He doesn't want you just to "cope." He wants you to have life, and freedom, and wonderful fulfillment in your life.

That life is in Jesus, for the Bible tells us, "And this is the record, that God hath given to us eternal life, and this life is in His Son" (I Jn. 5:11). And the power to live that life is found in the gift of the Holy Spirit ("But ye shall receive power, after the Holy Ghost is come upon you . . ." Acts 1:8). It is all as close as your breath — and just as free.

Yes, God loves you — completely — in spite of the fact that He knows all about you. You can't earn His love — nobody can — it's just that He can't help loving you! It's His nature. And He doesn't want you hurting; He doesn't want you to die.

The heart-cry of God was expressed through the prophet Ezekiel: ". . . for why will ye die, Oh house of Israel? For I have no pleasure in the death of him that dieth, saith the Lord: wherefore turn yourselves, and live ye" (Ezek. 18:31,32).

Are you tired, discouraged, sick in body,

heart or mind? Are you hungry for something that satisfies — something that works? Are you thirsty for the water of life, for spiritual reality, for that missing ingredient in your life?

God loves you, and because He does He has made perfect provision for your needs to be met — for the desires of your heart to be fulfilled. It is already prepared. And it is for you, whether you are an Isabel, a Frank or somewhere in between. No matter what you have done or not done, His hand is stretched out in love to you now.

"Come," God is saying to you now, "Come and live!"

# Chapter 2
# He Was There All The Time

"Behold, I stand at the door, and knock: if any man hear my voice, and open the door, I will come in to him, and will sup with him, and he with me."

(Rev. 3:20)

The Holy Spirit has always existed. To our finite minds that is incomprehensible. "Always" is infinite, and beyond our human ability to grasp; we can only accept it, and accept it we must. Because the Holy Spirit is God (I John 5:7; John 1:1), the third person of the Godhead has always existed. He makes His first appearance in the scriptures in the first chapter of the first book (Gen. 1:2), His last in the last chapter of the last book (Rev. 22:17) and, by virtue of His inspiration of the entire Bible (II Peter 1:21; II Tim. 3:16), He appears in every verse of every chapter of every book.

To so many of God's people the Holy Spirit is known only as part of the Doxology and of the Gloria Patri which they regularly sing, and of the Creeds which they recite. To many sincere, dedicated church people, the fact that the Holy Spirit is a life-giving, life-transforming, miracle-working force readily available to every hungry seeker seems to have been a carefully guarded secret. But He was there all the time, pursuing each lost and needy person, patiently waiting to be recognized and sought for, anxious to touch each of us with life in the Spirit. He was there all the time to grant to each believer the power from on high, and anxious to impart spiritual gifts as tools and weapons for His Church.

**The Mystery of the Godhead**

To most of us with traditional backgrounds it has always been relatively easy to visualize

18

God the father — often as a large, wise, kingly, old figure with a white beard, seated on a golden throne. Whether our image is accurate or not, the fact remains that most of us were able to conceive of Him in a definite way. Likewise, and much more accurately, we have been able to visualize God the Son in the form of Jesus the man. That's easy. But why has it been so difficult — if not impossible — to visualize and comprehend the third person of the Godhead, God the Holy Spirit? Why has He seemed so comparatively elusive and unreal? I believe it is because Jesus revealed the Father to us (John 15:26), as have the eyewitnesses who were with Him during His ministry on Earth (II Peter 1:16-18; I John 1:1-3). But the Holy Spirit seems to have no revealer. He is to be experienced daily, but it seems that God has not seen fit to provide a revealer of Him in the way that the Father and Son are revealed to us.

And there has been so little teaching in most traditional churches concerning the Holy Spirit. When Paul went to Ephesus and found a small group of disciples there he seemed to sense that something was missing in their lives. He asked them "Have ye received the Holy Ghost since ye believed?" And they replied "we have not so much as heard whether there be any Holy Ghost" (Acts 19:2). I believe this scene could take place in a great

19

many of our churches today. Is it reminiscent of your church? Have you ever wondered why?

## But Where Was God?

God created us for fellowship, and His availability to us through the course of human history seems to have depended upon the human condition — that is, on the amount of light man was willing to walk in. The following is an incomplete, but useful, outline that will help us to see how our own experience of God fits into the history of mankind.

**a. In the Garden.** Before sin entered the earth with the willful disobedience of Adam, man seems to have enjoyed perfect, close, uncomplicated fellowship with God the Father, apparently walking and talking with Him in the paradise environment God had created for him (Gen. 1:27; 3:10). But man sinned, died spiritually, and made that perfect relationship impossible (Hab. 1:13).

**b. Under the Old Covenant.** Under the Old Covenant, everyone knew where God was. There was no speculation, there was no inquiring or disputing. Everyone knew. God was between the cherubim, over the Ark of the Covenant, in the Holy of Holies, which was inside the Holy Place, which was inside the Court of the Congregation (Tabernacle), which was in their camp and was moved with them wherever they went. It was no secret — everyone knew (even the pagans knew).

But there was a problem. Because of the contamination with sin they could not approach God, except for one man. He was the High Priest, and even he could enter the Holy of Holies and approach God's presence only once a year; and then he could enter only after elaborate cleansing and preparation. And, not only that, but if he did it wrong he would die as he encountered the unimaginable purity of God's presence. It wasn't much, but it was the best man could do at the time (you might say it was the best God could do for man, given the state of man at that time).

**c. During the Life of Jesus on Earth.** For those 33 remarkable years, God walked the Earth in the form of Jesus of Nazareth, the eternal living Word, the Creator of the Universe, God the Son (John 1:1-3,14; John 17:5), being at the same time both God and man. For those who received and believed Him, to know and experience God was simply to know and experience Jesus.

**d. During the New Covenant Period.** When Jesus left the Earth, having established the Church and returned to His place in Heaven with the Father, He graciously sent the Third Person of the Godhead, God the Holy Spirit, to be God's abiding presence on Earth (John 14:15-18). Throughout the Church Age (New Covenant period) it seems to be true that

God's provision for our experience of Him is in the person of His Holy Spirit.

Now do you see the whole picture a little more clearly? And now do you see more clearly the importance of understanding the Holy Spirit of God? If you would know and experience God the Father today, you must know and experience His Spirit. If you would know and experience the Son today, you must know and experience His Spirit.

And this knowing and experiencing of the Spirit of God is for <u>you</u>. He loves you and intensely wants to redeem and to bless you. He really does.

# Chapter 3
# The Gift Is For Everyone

"And the gift is unto you, and to your children, and to all that are afar off, even as many as the Lord our God shall call."

(Acts 2:39)

## It's Really Simple

The life that God has prepared for you is to be found only in Jesus. It is only by coming to

Him - personally - that one can be reconciled to God and receive life - life in your spirit, imparted by the Holy Spirit (Jn. 14:6; I Jn. 5:11, 12; I Cor. 12:13).

But, once we are brought to a right relationship with God through the Lord Jesus Christ and born into His Kingdom, there is a life to be lived. The power necessary for living this wonderful life can only be had in the gift of the Holy Spirit.

In other words, the doorway through which we enter into this wonderful life is Jesus, God's only begotten Son. The key to living this life effectively and victoriously, once obtained, is the power Jesus imparts in the Gift of the Holy Spirit (Acts 1:8).

It's just that simple. Now - let's see how this all goes together.

**The Way It Was**

The Holy Spirit has always been the source of power in the lives of the people of God. This has been so from the beginning. But under the Old Covenant it seems that the Holy Spirit as an anointing, as a special enduement with power, was granted only to certain selected individuals such as the prophets, judges and kings (Jer. 1:4-10; Judges 15:14,15; I Sam. 16:13). And what is more, it seems that they could lose the anointing after it was conferred. We read in I Samuel that the Holy Spirit came upon David when Samuel anointed him with oil, and remained with him from that day on. Yet after his fall into sin concerning Bathsheba and Uriah the Hittite, David pleaded with God to "Take not thy Holy Spirit from me" (Ps. 51:11). Saul, Israel's first King, was anointed by Samuel and the Spirit came upon him (I Sam. 10:1-9); yet, after repeatedly turning away from God's commandments and doing things his own way, the Holy Spirit was taken from him and madness seems to have tormented him from that day on.

During the earthly ministry of Jesus, He conferred limited, or temporary, anointing with the Holy Spirit's power to His disciples in order for them to carry out the missions to which He assigned them (Luke 9:1-6; Luke 10:1-20). But it truly seems to have been limited and temporary.

**The Way It Was Going To Be**

Sometime between 400 and 800 B.C. (no one seems to know exactly when the prophet Joel lived, but most authorities believe it was within this span of time) Joel prophesied. He said the day was coming when the anointing of the Holy Spirit would be poured out upon all sorts of people - not just selected Hebrew leaders, not even just all Hebrews, but on all types of people of all nations of the Earth, even on the most lowly - on servants and slaves. He prophesied "And it shall come to pass afterward, that I will pour out my Spirit upon all flesh; and your sons and your daughters shall prophesy, your old men shall dream dreams, your young men shall see visions: And also upon the servants and upon the handmaids in those days will I pour out my spirit" (Joel 2:28,29). These were radical words that fell upon those Jewish ears! I don't think very many believed them at the time. Not only would their sons prophesy, but also their daughters! Not only would God's Spirit be poured out on wealthy Arabs, Greeks and Africans, but also on their servants and slaves! And this was approximately **600** years before the birth of the One who would do the pouring (Acts 2:32,33).

During the earthly ministry of Jesus, the time was drawing near.

## The Way It Is

This outpouring of God's Spirit on the day of Pentecost (Acts 2) marked the beginning of the period about which Joel spoke. There can be no doubt about this, for Peter stood up that day and declared that the outpouring they were seeing, hearing and experiencing was just that (Acts 2:14-21). Then he went on to say, in case there could be any doubt, that the gift being received would be for all God's people, across the centuries to come (Acts 2:38,39).

And what is even more wonderful, this precious gift seems to be <u>permanent</u> (John 14:16). We can lose our <u>awareness</u> of God's presence by allowing sin to remain in our lives (Is. 59:1,2); we can spoil the quality of our fellowship with Him (Hab. 1:13); but He will <u>never</u> depart from us (Hebr. 13:5) and it seems that the gifts and callings of God, once granted, are never withdrawn from us (Rom. 11:29).

Isn't that a radical change? And isn't it good news?

### And It's A Gift

It is terribly important to know, and to remember, that this wonderful granting of God's Holy Spirit is a <u>gift</u>. We cannot earn it, nor can we ever deserve it; if it could be earned it wouldn't be a gift, it would be a reward. Then we would be proud of it.

God doesn't reward us with it because we have earned it, for what we <u>really deserve</u>, what we have really <u>earned</u>, even the "best" of us, is judgment and destruction (Rom. 3:23: Rom. 6:23). No - no one could earn it; don't try to. Just acknowledge that it is a wonderful, gracious gift, freely bestowed, and appreciate Him for it.

The happy fact is that He freely gives it to us, not because we deserve it, but in spite of the fact that we <u>don't</u> deserve it. Get hold of that wonderful truth; it's a <u>gift</u>! And He gives it to us because He loves us and knows that we need it.

## But Don't All Christians Have the Holy Spirit

Christians sometimes fuss over this question. I like to put it this way: all Christians have the Holy Spirit, but the Holy Spirit doesn't have all Christians. Surely the Holy Spirit, in a measure, comes and indwells our spirits at the time of the new birth (Rom. 8:9-11). But it is also clear that we can be born-again believers with the indwelling presence of the Holy Spirit and still need, in addition, the fullness of His power which only comes with being filled and completely surrendered in the baptism with His Spirit and power. This will be pursued thoroughly in Chapter 6, but for now you can see a clear illustration of this in Acts 8:5-17. The Samaritan people had accepted Jesus as savior and been baptized in water; yet it still remained for Peter and John to go down to Samaria and pray for them to receive this power.

Yes, God loves you - without measure; and He wants to give you His spirit - without measure.

# Chapter 4
# Do We
# Really Need It?

"And being assembled together with them, (Jesus) commanded them that they should not depart from Jerusalem, but wait for the promise of the Father, which, saith He, ye have heard of me."

(Acts 1:4)

## The Promise Is To You

The promise of God is that He <u>will</u> give you

the power of the Holy Spirit to transform your life. "The promise is unto you, and to your children, and to all that are afar off, even as many as the Lord our God shall call" (Acts 2:39). So you <u>don't</u> have to struggle through life, never as effective as you want to be, never achieving victory, fulfillment and satisfaction in your life. You don't have to live that way. The power <u>is</u> for you, for your achievement and satisfaction, to the glory of God (Matt. 5:16) — not just for the performance of specific ministries within the Church, but in everything you do, every day. Your life should be so different that you shine as a light in darkness (Phil. 2:15, 16). Then people will want to know how you got that way. You will be a witness unto Him (Acts 1:8).

## The Heartbreak of God

If you want to <u>really</u> hurt someone's feelings, a sure way to do it is to wait until he has purchased a wonderful gift for you — sacrificed in order to purchase it — and then, out of a heart of love, presents this gift to you. Then tell him you don't want it. That really hurts!

I believe the great heartbreak of God is not so much the sin of the sinner as it is the self-satisfied indifference of the saint, willing to have so little of God and for God to have so little of him. As a friend of mine has expressed in a song, "God has feelings too", and it seems certain that His children hurt Him badly in this way.

## But Is It Important?

Jesus never wasted a word. This must be true for I know that he never sinned (II Cor. 5:21), and speaking idle words is apparently a sin (Matt 12:36). I believe that everything Jesus said on Earth was important. Surely, then, the last words He spoke on earth, knowing full well that they would be His last words to His disciples on Earth, were extremely important. You see, He knew it would be his very last opportunity to speak to His followers before He had to return to the Father in Heaven, leaving this difficult, diverse group of fishermen, tax collectors and others with little in common to go on without Him and establish the Kingdom. Surely, what He said would be of great importance. It was.

**The Last Word.** When my children are leaving the house for school, I have one last opportunity to tell them something as they run for the bus. I can call to them as they go, but it will be my last opportunity to influence them in this way until the end of the day. I may call after them something like "Don't forget to give that note to the principal" or "Don't forget that you have a piano lesson after school." Whatever I tell them, it will be the thing I consider most important — the one thing, above all else, that I want to leave fresh in their awareness. It is my last chance to directly influence them before they are out of my reach for a period of time.

And what Jesus said, the thing He wanted to leave ringing in their minds as He was taken up to leave them for about 2,000 years, was a simple command to "tarry ye in the city of Jerusalem, until ye be endued with power* from on high" (Luke 24:49). A more complete account of this same final conversation is found in Acts chapter one, and we find there that with the command Jesus included a precious promise. "And, being assembled together with them, commanded them that they should not depart from Jerusalem, but wait for the promise of the Father, which, saith He, ye have heard of me. For John truly baptized with water, but ye shall be baptized with the Holy Ghost not many days hence" (Acts 1:4,5).

Now, it appears to me that the followers of Jesus never really understood who He was, or what He was attempting to do, until Pentecost. They did not yet have the spiritual insight and understanding they needed, for the abiding

---

*The Greek word translated "power" here (and in Acts 1:8) is "dunamis" and is the word from which we derive such English words as dynamite, dynamic, and dynamo. It means power — power that does things, moves things, changes things — power that gets results.

presence of the Holy Spirit had not yet been manifested in their lives (John 14:16,26). They were competing and striving for position and favor with Him in a most carnal way, even at the very end (Matt. 20:20-24). They just didn't understand. And at this point, with priceless pearls of eternal truth pouring from the Master's lips, they interrupted Him with a silly, irrelevant question (v. 6). And Jesus, with His wonderful patience, answered their silly question (v. 7) and then returned to what He wanted them to hear in those closing seconds of His physical presence on Earth. He said "But ye shall receive power, after that the Holy Ghost is come upon you; and ye shall be witnesses unto me . . ." (v. 8). The following verse makes it clear that these were the final seconds of His physical presence on Earth: "And when He had spoken these things, while they beheld, He was taken up; and a cloud received Him out of their sight."

So is this receiving of power of which Jesus spoke important? Yes — infinitely important — to you, to the Lord Jesus Christ and to His Kingdom.

**Consider Jesus**

It seems clear that even the Lord Himself required the power of the Holy Spirit in order to fulfill His earthly ministry. This may seem to you like a radical statement, but it seems clear that Jesus did all the things He did on Earth as a man, with every human limitation, anointed with this enabling power from on high.

**Consider the Scriptural Record.** There is no record of any miraculous acts by the Lord until after the Spirit descended and remained upon Him at the time of His water baptism in the Jordan (John 1:29-34). You may look, but it simply isn't there.

Then read in Luke 4:1 "And Jesus <u>being full of the Holy Ghost</u> returned from (the) Jordan - - -". He was immediately taken into the wilderness and overcame the devil's temptations for forty days without food. And. at the end of this trial of trials, rather than staggering out, victorious but spent, we find in verses 13 and 14, "And when the devil had ended all the temptation, he departed from Him for a season. And Jesus returned <u>in the power of the Spirit</u> into Galilee - - -". He had received the power from the Father and was on the move!

Finally, consider the way Peter declared Him to those at the house of Cornelius. He told them, "<u>How God anointed Jesus of Nazareth with the Holy Ghost and with power:</u> who went about doing good, and healing all who were oppressed of the devil; for God was with Him" (Acts 10:38). Peter didn't say He did these things because He was God (although He surely was, is and ever shall be God); rather he said clearly that Jesus did these things because He was anointed with the Holy Ghost and power, and because God was <u>with Him</u>.

## Consider the Fruit

The followers of Jesus all had deserted Him during His final hours of betrayal, agony and death (Mk. 14:50). By the time Jesus gave them this last command with its promise and ascended into Heaven before their eyes, the entire company of followers numbered only about 120. Yet that small band, so troublesome and unpromising before, once endued with this power that Jesus promised, blazed the message of Jesus around the world, enduring hardship, persecution, torture and martyrdom, and changed the course of history forever.

That's fruit.

## Consider Peter

Peter, on the night Jesus was betrayed, had denied three separate times that he even knew Him. He denied and cursed his Lord, just to save his own skin. Yet this same Peter, within <u>minutes</u> of receiving the power from on high, went down into the street, faced a jeering, hostile mob, boldly proclaimed this same Jesus and 3,000 people repented and were born into the Kingdom of God! How can we explain this? What brought about the remarkable change in Peter? Jesus explained it in advance when He said to them, ten days earlier, that they were not to leave town, not to try to preach, heal the sick, cast out devils. They were not to go ahead on their own and try to repeat the mission journeys they had already taken for and with Him. He told them they needed the <u>power</u> of the Holy Spirit, and that when they had received that power <u>then</u> they would become witnesses unto Him, from Jerusalem, even to the rest of the world. <u>That's how we explain "the new Peter".</u> He had been empowered and transformed by the Holy Spirit and, as a result, had become a most effective witness.

Just like Jesus said he would.

**Consider Foreign Missions Results Today**

It is a matter of common knowledge and public record that the only Christian groups experiencing consistent success on the foreign mission fields in terms of numbers of lost people brought into the kingdom, new churches established and growth in existing churches are the groups which acknowledge and receive this power Jesus spoke of. Missionary Jim Montgomery, in his book "Fire in the Philippines"*, tells how he went to the Philippines convinced that he didn't need this gift of

---

*Montgomery, Jim: <u>Fire in the Philippines</u>, Creation House, Carol Stream, IL., 1975

the Holy Spirit. He had been told that Spirit-filled missionaries were shallow, uncommitted thrill-seekers who were not effective on the field. But after he had been there a while he compared the results (fruit) achieved by six "pentecostal" or "charismatic" denominational groups with those achieved by six non-pentecostal denominational groups which had been in the Philippines for about the same length of time. He discovered that the "pentecostal" or "charismatic" groups had <u>thirty-six</u> times the number of converts! Imagine that . . . . <u>thirty-six</u> lost people reached for Jesus and born into the Kingdom for every <u>one</u> reached and won by the non-pentecostal groups! What makes the difference in these two groups of missionaries is apparently the same thing that made the difference between the old Peter and the new Peter: the gift of the Holy Spirit and the resulting power. That's what Jesus said would happen.

## Consider the Attitude of Jesus

It's interesting to me that the word used in Acts 1:4 is "commanded". He didn't <u>suggest</u> that they needed this power; He didn't say that their ministries might be more productive if they would receive it; He didn't say that it was an unimportant option that they could elect to accept or reject. No, He <u>commanded</u> them to stay right where they were until they received it. And the Greek word used here for "commanded" is a military term used to describe an order issued by a superior officer which must be obeyed. Jesus knew they needed it, and He commanded them to wait in Jerusalem until they received it.

## Consider the Contemporary Church at Home

Is the established Church where you live setting the World ablaze with the wonderful Gospel of salvation? Is it a powerful, dynamic, tradition-shaking, life-changing force in your community? Is it? There is a game show on television which is a word-association game. The producers poll a large number of people, asking them to name the word most closely associated with the game word. Their answers are compiled, and the consensus of their opinions becomes the "correct" answer in the game. Then, on the show, the contestant is given the game word and asked to state the word he most closely associates with it; if the contestant chooses the same word as the consensus of the population sample, he wins. Not long ago, on the show, the game word was "boring". The correct answer, as derived from the opinions of the people polled, was "church". How sad this must make the Lord, who established the church with Himself as its Head, endowed it with supernatural, miracle-working power and sent it against a supernatural enemy to conquer and change the world forever. Yet, now, in many people's minds, "church" equates to "boring".

## What the Church Needs Now

What the church needs today, if we are to win the World for Jesus, is not so much apostolic succession, as apostolic success. If we are to have apostolic success, we need apostolic power. And if we are to have apostolic power we need the apostolic baptism by Jesus in the Holy Spirit.

Jesus said so.

## Consider Yourself

One reason so many priests and ministers are giving up in discouragement, frustration and disillusionment is that they are trying to do the work of God without the power of God. One reason that our non-Christian neighbors are not attracted to Jesus is because they see no more victory, effectiveness and joy in our lives than they have in their own; perhaps they sometimes see less. Those disciples of Jesus had seen and experienced His earthly ministry. They had been with Him through it all. They had even healed the sick, cast out demons and, apparently, raised the dead themselves (Matt. 10:1-8)! Still He told them they weren't ready to go into the field of ministry yet because they lacked the power. Let's be reasonable: if <u>they</u> needed it, don't <u>you</u>?

# Chapter 5
# Jesus The Baptizer

"... there cometh One mightier than I after me, the latchet of whose shoes I am not worthy to stoop down and unloose. I indeed have baptized you with water: but He shall baptize you with the Holy Ghost."

(Mk. 1:7,8)

I remember the first time I ever heard the expression "baptism in the Holy Spirit." It was after Sunday services at the Ranch House Chapel, Camp Pendleton, California. We were having tea and cookies on the patio (we called it "fellowship") and a lady named Judy, newly arrived with her husband there for duty, introduced herself. In the course of the conversation she told me that she had been baptized in the Holy Spirit. I said, "How nice." I hadn't the slightest idea what she was talking about; I just thought she was a little strange.

In retrospect, it is remarkable that this expression was meaningless to me, for I had studied the New Testament. Surely I had seen it many times, for it appears in all four gospels and the Book of Acts; yet it had never penetrated my awareness. There seem to have been many others like me, yet it has been there all along, plain as can be. There is such a baptism, and Jesus is the Baptizer.

When Jesus came to John in the Jordan to be baptized in water, John, inspired by the Holy Spirit, declared "I indeed baptize you in water unto repentance: but He that cometh after me is mightier than I, whose shoes I am not worthy to bear: He shall baptize you with the Holy Ghost, and with fire;" (Matt. 3:11). This is repeated in Mk. 1:7,8 and Luke 3:16. These passages establish that there is such a thing as being baptized in (or with) the Holy Spirit, and strongly infer that it is Jesus who performs this baptism. In John's account (John

42

1:29-34) any doubt about the identity of Jesus as the Holy Spirit Baptizer is removed, for John the Baptist is recorded as saying, "And I saw, and bear record that this is the Son of God." Then Jesus, in those last instructions to His disciples, identified the experience they were to receive as the baptism in the Holy Spirit: "Wait for the promise of the Father, which, saith He, ye have heard of Me. For John truly baptized with water, but ye shall be baptized with the Holy Ghost not many days hence" (Acts 1:4,5). Then, on the day of Pentecost, Peter confirmed that the outpouring was the work of Jesus: "Therefore being by the right hand of God exalted, and having received of the Father the promise of the Holy Ghost, He hath shed forth this, which ye now see and hear" (Acts 2:33).

**But What Do We Call It?**

At this point it may be useful to point out that this same gift of power is called by several names in the New Testament. In addition to the baptism in (with) the Holy Spirit, it is referred to as the promise of the Father (Lk. 24:49; Acts 1:4); the gift of the Holy Spirit (Acts 2:38; 10:45); being filled with the Holy Spirit (Acts 8:15,17; 19:2); and having the Holy Spirit fall upon the believer (Acts 10:44). There seem to be a number of Christians who are uncomfortable with the expression "baptism in the Holy Spirit"; often they have said to me "It's alright to speak of being "filled" with the Holy Spirit, just don't say "baptized". But I find no scriptural basis for that; it was good enough for Jesus, John the Baptist, Matthew, Mark, Luke, John, and Peter, and who am I to correct them? As a matter of fact, the expression seems to have been originated by God the Father, for John the Baptist said that the One (God the Father) who had sent him to baptize in water had told him that the One on whom he saw the Spirit descending and remaining (Jesus) would be the One who would "baptize with the Holy Ghost" (John 1:32-34).

So it seems entirely scriptural to speak of this gift as the baptism in the Holy Spirit, but the other ways of expressing it are valid also.

It really doesn't matter so much what we call it, as long as we acknowledge and receive it.

### But What About This Baptism Of Fire?

In both Matthew's (Matt. 3:12) and Luke's (Lk. 3:17) accounts of John the Baptist's annunciation of Jesus as the Baptizer in the Holy Spirit, the words "and fire" are added. That seems, most unmistakably, to say that Jesus is also the One who confers the "baptism of fire". But what is that? The baptism of (with) fire is less well understood than the baptism in the Holy Spirit (and much less popular); but it seems to be a purging process by means of which Jesus identifies the chaff (the things in our lives that don't please Him, and don't help us or others) and <u>burns</u> it out of our lives. It usually hurts, but always leaves us better off, more free, and more like Him. And it seems to go on, more or less indefinitely, as long as there is any chaff left in us, for He says the fire is "unquenchable."

This purging, this purifying with the fire of God, may begin at the new birth; for some believers it does, most noticeably. But, at the very least, it is intensified with the receiving of the baptism in the Holy Spirit. Typically, the believer newly baptized in the Holy Spirit becomes a great deal more sensitive to sin in his own life. I believe this has a great deal to do with the distinct emphasis within pentecostal or charismatic groups on personal holiness. Am I saying that Spirit-baptized Christians are always more holy than other Christians? Not at all. However, <u>as a group</u> they tend to be more sensitive to the need for personal holiness, and more sensitive to sin in their own lives. Thus, I believe, has come the emphasis on holiness in their teaching and preaching, along with the tendency of other Christians to refer to them as "holiness" groups.

At Pentecost one of the supernatural events was the appearance of tongues of fire which "sat upon each of them" (Acts 2:3). The fire apparently represented this aspect of the Lord's gift. It is interesting to note that there was no such fire in the case of Jesus in the Jordan —

only the heavenly Dove. This, of course, would be true of Him because He was sinless, with nothing to be burned out. He got only the Dove; but we get the Dove <u>and</u> the fire. Count on it!

## A Helpful Comparison

It is helpful, in trying to understand the baptism in the Holy Spirit, to compare it with the baptism in water.

In water baptism the baptizer is some other Christian (often your pastor); the medium (the thing you are baptized in) is water - natural, plain water. And the purpose of water baptism, basically, is to enter into the death, burial, and resurrection of Jesus — to put to death and bury the old nature and be clothed in His nature (Rom. 6:3-11; Gal. 3:27; Col. 2:10-12).

In Holy Spirit baptism the Baptizer is Jesus (how He comes from Heaven to do it I do not know — I only know that He does); the medium is the Holy Spirit — <u>living</u> water (Jn. 4:10-14; 7:37-39); and the purpose is to receive power for service, power for living. So this power comes with the baptism <u>by</u> Jesus, <u>in</u> the Holy Spirit.

And if you know Him as savior it is for you. He is the only one who does it — there is no other Holy Spirit baptizer — and He wants to do it for you.

# Chapter 6
# The New Testament Pattern

"When they heard this, they were baptized in the name of the Lord Jesus. And when Paul had laid his hands upon them, the Holy Ghost came upon them; and they spake with tongues, and prophesied."

(Acts 19:5,6)

## A Word of Caution

It seems to be natural for men to want to

make rules. We are inclined to systematize and doctrinalize almost everything, including our experience of God, and His provision for us. We seem to find some sort of false security in deciding how God should behave, and then making rules to that effect. In most of our churches we have rules for almost everything. And the more I learn of God, the more sure I am that He is not the least bit impressed with our rules. In fact, I suspect that He has a wonderful time doing things that don't fit our traditions; He seems to delight in breaking our rules. So beware of that which insists "if you want to be acceptable to God, you must do this, this and this, and you certainly must not do that," or "before you can receive this from God, you must first do this and receive that." God is not legalistic; in fact, He is delightfully, refreshingly flexible and, in a sense, unpredictable.

At this point some may bristle, stiffen their necks, prepare to burn the book and say something like "God is not unpredictable! He honors His Word and always operates according to it." Hang on now — don't burn the book — I agree with you. He does honor His Word, even above His Name (Ps. 138:2); His Word is unchanging, standard forever (Ps. 12:6,7; Is. 40:8) and He chooses always to abide by it. But our traditions, rules and doctrines are not the Word of God. So beware of rules and doctrines which say that

God will only act in this way or that, or only after you have performed certain pre-requisites. Be careful of such narrowness; at best it is risky, and it can be bondage.

## But There Are Patterns

And yet it is useful to see that there are some scriptural patterns for the life of the believer. One such pattern is the pattern of growth in the lives of New Testament converts — the new Christians of the first century. As always, there are individual exceptions; but if we study the New Testament as a whole, there emerges a general pattern which is useful for us to see. The typical New Testament believer seems to have heard the Good News, accepted Jesus as the Messiah, been born into the Kingdom, baptized in water and baptized in the Holy Spirit — usually in that order, and often all in the same day. (See Acts 8:5-17 and Acts 19:1-6)

## And There Are Some Who Disagree

At this point I suppose I should say that there are some sincere Christians who believe that the baptism by Jesus in the Holy Spirit is not a valid experience for our day. I used to believe that because I was taught to believe that. But now that I have studied the matter carefully for ten years I cannot find one line of Scripture, nor even a single scrap of logic, to support that belief.* There are more lost people in the world today than there were in the first century and the great commission is far from being fulfilled (Matt. 28:18-20; Mark 16:15-20). Why would God withdraw the power necessary for fulfilling the Great Commission so many centuries before it is fulfilled? To believe such a notion we would have to abandon reason and remove vast portions of our Bibles. I have no intention of doing either one.

## Do We Get It All When We're Saved?

Then there are others who will say that it all happens when you are born again. This belief is usually anchored in I Cor. 12:13 "for by one Spirit we are all baptized into one Body." But this is a baptism by the Holy Spirit into the Body of Christ (read the verse carefully). This is Salvation; this is the new birth, by means of which the Holy Spirit, the Agent and Force of our salvation, cleanses us and carries us through the Gate (Jesus) into the Body of Christ. But the baptism we speak of, this induement with power for service, is the baptism by Jesus, in the Holy Spirit. If this seems confusing to you just remember Who the baptizer is in each case, and the result or purpose. Remember the distinction: the identity of the baptizer in each case, and the pur-

*To fully explain and document this fact would take much too much space here. You may request the cassette tape on this subject, HS 1 — "Why These Things Have Not Passed Away", which discusses it fully with many scripture references.

pose or result. They cannot be the same.

This difference of opinion is going on, and needs to be dealt with. To those who say that there is no such separate experience, that "you get it all when you are saved" one might respond with a question: "If you got it all when you were saved, where is it?" Are they, like Paul, carrying forth the wonderful Gospel of salvation, "not with enticing words of man's wisdom, but in <u>demonstration</u> of the Spirit and of <u>power</u>" (I Cor. 2:4)? We might well ask the question, but it alone wouldn't really address the issue in a constructive way. Let us rather examine the scriptural record.

## The Original Disciples at Pentecost

Jesus told the original disciples that they must tarry in Jerusalem until they had received the baptism in the Holy Spirit. Surely they were "children of God by faith in Christ Jesus" (Gal. 3:26). They had healed the sick, cleansed lepers, cast out demons and probably raised the dead — all in the name of Jesus (Matt. 10:7,8; Lk. 9:1,2; 10:1,17). Surely these, gathered later in the upper room on the day of Pentecost, were not unregenerate Jews. Yet those who deny this baptism by Jesus must explain Pentecost somehow, and they usually say that those original disciples were just being converted, just being saved on the day of Pentecost. Yet Jesus told them much earlier, in Luke 10:20, that they should rejoice because their names were "written in Heaven." Throughout the Bible, to have your name written in Heaven means to be a child of God, it means sonship, it means salvation (Ex. 32:32; Ps. 69:28; Phil. 4:3; Rev. 3:5; Rev. 20:15; Rev. 21:27, etc.). If that's not enough, the resurrected, glorified Jesus, after Calvary, breathed on them in John 20:22 and said "Receive ye the Holy Ghost"; and apparently Jesus had earlier baptised them in water. Surely there can be no doubt that they were born-again Christians, not unredeemed Jews. Yet 40 days after the resurrection He told them they must wait in the city until they had been baptized in the Holy Spirit. Ten days after that, on the Day of Pentecost, they did receive this baptism of power, and the transformation wrought in them is a matter of history.

**The Revival in Samaria**

After the martyrdom of Stephen (Acts 6:8 - 7:60), Philip went down to Samaria and preached Jesus to them in the power of the Holy Spirit (Acts 8:5-25). He cast out evil spirits and the sick were healed. Because he preached "in the demonstration of the Spirit and of power" the people listened to the Good News. See this, please; it is so important that you see it. The only reason that those pagans even listened to his preaching — those pagans, completely dominated by, and under the power of, a magician named Simon the Sorcerer (Acts 8:9-11) — the only reason they even listened to the preaching of the gospel was because of the miracle-working power of the Holy Spirit demonstrated before them. Read verses 6 and 7: "And the people with one accord gave heed unto those things which Philip spake, hearing and seeing the miracles which he did. For unclean spirits, crying with loud voice, came out of many that were possessed with them: and many taken with palsies, and that were lame, were healed."

Now, read verses 12 through 17 and you see that the people believed on Jesus, then were baptized in His name in water, and yet — subsequently — Peter and John came down from Jerusalem, prayed for them and laid their hands on them so they would "receive the Holy Ghost". If this receiving of the Holy Ghost came automatically with receiving Jesus and being baptized in water, then Peter and John wasted a trip. But of course they didn't waste the trip; they knew exactly what they were doing. They went to Samaria, gathered those new Christians together, prayed for them, laid their hands on them and then those new Christians received this gift, this baptism in the Holy Spirit. It was the typical New Testament pattern: they heard the gospel preached with power, received Jesus as their savior, were baptized in water and then were baptized in the Holy Spirit — in that order.

## Saul the Persecutor Becomes
## Paul the Christian

When Saul of Tarsus, that pharisee of pharisees, that hater of Jesus, that zealous, committed persecutor of the Church, was struck down on the road to Damascus I believe he was converted, or redeemed, there. I believe he was born into the Kingdom there in that blinding presence of Jesus, for he twice called Jesus "Lord" (Acts 9:1-6), and the Bible says "no man can say that Jesus is the Lord, but by the Holy Ghost" (I Cor. 12:3). Yet three days later, as Saul obeyed Jesus, fasting and praying, the Lord sent an obscure disciple named Ananias to him, to lay his hands upon Saul so that he might receive his sight "and be filled with the Holy Ghost." Then, immediately after being healed and filled with the Holy Spirit, Saul was baptized in water. It must be true that Saul the Persecutor accepted Jesus as Lord and became Saul the Redeemed there on the Damascus road, for he not only called Jesus "Lord" (once after Jesus had identified Himself to Saul), but he immediately obeyed the One he had previously hated and fought so bitterly, and began to fast and pray. Also, notice that when Ananias first arrived, operat-

54

ing under divine revelation, he first (before he touched him or prayed) called him "brother Saul."

Once this is studied with any care, and without a closed mind, it is clear that Saul was first born into the Kingdom; then, three days later, he was filled with the Holy Spirit, healed and then baptized in water.

The Lord rearranged the sequence of events here; He will not be confined by our doctrines.

## Salvation Comes to the Household of a Roman Officer

Some time after the conversion, empowering and baptism of Saul of Tarsus, the Lord sent Peter to the home of a gentile, a Roman officer named Cornelius. It wasn't easy for the Lord to get Peter to go. It went against everything that strong-willed Jew had ever been taught (it was a violation of the Jewish law even to go into a gentile's house — let alone to preach to them and invite them to become children of God there). The Lord had to send angels, visions (He repeated Peter's vision three times) and give supernatural confirmation, just to get Peter to go into that gentile's house. Then, as Peter preached, the Holy Spirit fell upon all the household who heard the Word preached, and they were born again (I Cor. 12:13) and baptized in the Holy Spirit

(Acts 2:4) while Peter was still preaching. It must have been perplexing for Peter; he hadn't even given the altar call yet! (Acts 10:44). Because Peter and the Jewish Christians with him realized that those pagans had actually been saved and baptized in the Holy Spirit, they consented to baptize them in water. (Baptizing those "pagans" in water got Peter in trouble with the other elders in Jerusalem, and he successfully defended himself in Acts 11, settling the issue for all time). Here again the Lord rearranged the sequence; he apparently did it because He knew Peter would never baptize them in water if he hadn't first been convinced that they were Christians by their receiving the baptism in the Holy Spirit, just as they had received on the day of Pentecost (Acts 10:45-47; 11:15,16).

Incidentally, the Lord probably also knew that it would be awfully difficult to get Peter to lay his Jewish hands on those gentile heads. There were limits, after all, to what can be expected of a man, so He just went ahead and poured the Holy Spirit out upon them without any laying-on of hands. God is so good, and He always has a way!

**The Establishment of the Church at Ephesus**
After leaving Corinth, Paul went to Ephesus and found a small number of disciples who had apparently come to the Lord

under the ministry of Appollos, Aquila and Priscilla. But he seems to have sensed that there was something missing in them, and asked them "Have ye received the Holy Ghost since ye believed?" He discovered that they knew nothing of the Holy Spirit's power, and had only received the water baptism of John the Baptist. After Paul explained, they were baptized "in the name of the Lord Jesus", and then (subsequently) Paul laid his hands upon them and they received this enduement with Holy Ghost power (Acts 19:2-6).

## All Things Considered

Please don't try to make a doctrine of this, but when we consider all the New Testament accounts, there seems to be a general pattern for new believers.* They usually believed the good news, received Jesus as Messiah/Savior, were baptized in water and then received the baptism in the Holy Spirit, often all in the same day.

And that's the way it happened. Don't make your decisions on the basis of traditions, opinions (no matter how widely accepted, or by whom), not even the lives of Godly people

---

*There are some who insist that we may not use the Book of Acts as a basis for our beliefs and doctrines — that we rather must trust only the writings of Paul. But when we study the writings of Paul, we find him saying that we may use all scriptures for this purpose: "All scripture is given by inspiration of God, and is profitable for doctrine . . ." II Tim. 3:16.

dear to you. The only sure and safe basis, the only unchanging standard, is the Word of God. Settle for nothing less.

# Chapter 7
# Ye Must Be Born Again

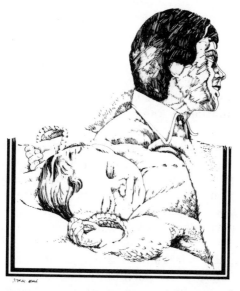

"That which is born of the flesh is flesh; and that which is born of the Spirit is spirit. Marvel not that I said unto thee, Ye must be born again."

(John 3:6,7)

There is only one prerequisite to receiving the gift of the Holy Spirit: you must be a Christian, born of the Spirit of God into His Kingdom by faith in Christ Jesus.

Many people who would read this far in such a book would probably say something like, "Of course I'm a Christian — my parents were Christians, I was reared in a Christian home and I have been in church all my life. Why even raise such a question?" I would have said the same thing for most of my life, and would have been grieved with you if you had even suggested that I was not a Christian. Yet I wasn't. I was like Nicodemus (John 3:1-7), religious but lost. I knew the church, I knew confirmation, I knew the sacraments. I took religion seriously — in the same way that I took patriotism, morality and Jeffersonian philosophy seriously. I taught Sunday school, I studied the Bible, I knew a good deal about Jesus; but I didn't know Jesus (the difference may seem slight, but it is actually infinite — it is everything). I was rightly related to the church's traditions and activities, but I was not rightly related to the Head of the Church. I didn't know Jesus personally, had never given Him my life, had never asked Him to bring life to my spirit and live there. I had experienced a natural birth — everyone has — but I had never experienced the supernatural birth. I knew the physical birth, but not the spiritual one.

I was just like Nicodemus. Are you? Could

it be that you have strived to please God all these years, worked hard in the church, but never really had that one-on-one encounter with Him to personally receive Him as savior and Lord of your life? If there is even a shadow of a doubt about that, get it resolved right now. Turn to Him personally and tell Him that you want to get it settled — once and forever.

## What Must We Do to be Saved?

At this point we may as well face an unhappy reality — different Christian groups have different opinions about what one must do to be born again. Some emphasize one thing and others emphasize another. But let's avoid that confusion. At the heart of it all there is one thing upon which Christians would all agree — one thing upon which it all depends. That "strait gate", that central point, that unavoidable, ultimate issue is this: what are you going to do about Jesus?

Jesus claimed to be the Messiah, the pre-existant Son of God (John 4:25,26; 8:58; 17:5), and the only means of salvation (John 14:6). If He is anything less we should dismiss Him as a liar or a lunatic; if He is who He claimed to be, we must acknowledge, accept and serve Him.

A great many people, especially those who consider themselves intellectual, cosmopolitan, thinking people, take a position concerning Jesus which goes more or less like this: "Jesus was a great man, a great prophet, a great teacher and a great humanitarian — perhaps the greatest who ever lived — and I honor him for that. But he certainly was not divine — he was not God." This position, however, is intellectually and logically impossible. No such valid position exists, for Jesus claimed to be God. If He is anything less, then He was not a great man, great prophet, great teacher, or great example to be followed. If He is not exactly who and what He claimed to be then he is a dead phony; there is no middle-ground alternative.

Jesus of Nazareth is either everything, or He is nothing. We must decide. This central, fundamental, ultimate issue is summed up in one verse: "He that hath the Son hath life; and he that hath not the Son of God hath not life." (I Jn. 5:12). Do you have Him? Do you have true spiritual life?

In order to be redeemed and born into the Kingdom you must believe that Jesus is the eternal Son of God, Savior of the World (John 3:16), that He is the only savior — the only way to the Father (John 14:6) and you must personally (no one can do it for you) receive Him into your life as Savior and King (John 1:11-13). Just believing in God is not nearly enough — even demons "also believe, and tremble" (Jas. 2:19). Even believing the claims of Jesus isn't enough — we must act. We must receive Him as Messiah, as Savior, as Lord (He will never force His way into our lives). In John 1:11,12 this is clearly revealed: "He came unto His own and His own received Him not. But as many as received Him, to them gave He power to become the sons (and daughters) of God, even to them that believed on His name."

Implicit in turning to Him and receiving Him as Lord is what the Bible calls repentance, which is a turning away from sin and death, for it is obvious that we cannot serve sin and serve the enemy of sin at the same time (Matthew 6:24; Romans 6:6). "Repent" means to turn around — to change directions. In the scriptural sense we must, by a deliberate act of the will, decide to turn away from sin and death, and turn to life and freedom. This is essential (Acts 2:38); this is so important that I will say it again: we cannot serve sin, and serve the enemy of sin, at the same time. When we decide to follow Jesus we necessarily decide not to follow sin and darkness. Jesus put it plainly and simply by saying that we cannot serve two masters — we must, like Joshua, choose whom we will serve (Matt. 6:24; Josh. 24:15).

## But What Does "Saved" Mean?

For most of my life, talk about being "saved" didn't mean anything to me. It sounded so unsophisticated, so shallow, so "red-neck." For someone to ask me a question like, "Brother are you saved?" just didn't bless me at all — nor did it convict me at all. I didn't know what "saved" meant (and, I suspect, neither do many of those who ask the question).

It seems to have been another of those carefully-guarded secrets about something wonderful; for the real meaning of "saved" is truly a wonderful thing, and it makes me wonder why someone didn't tell me about it long ago.

In the Greek language, in which the New Testament was originally written, the word translated "saved" is "sozo" and it is a marvelous word. "Sozo" actually means five things. It means: to be rescued; to be healed (physically and emotionally); to be delivered from demonic pressure, torment or bondage; to be caused to prosper; and to be made whole. Yes — it means all those things — and all five are the inheritance of the redeemed.

When you are born-again, all these wonderful aspects of being saved become yours by inheritance. It may take time for you to experience all of them and learn to walk in them daily; but legally they become yours when you are born into the Kingdom of God. And that really is good news!

## Get It Settled

If you are not certain, if you should die right this moment with this book before your eyes, that you would be with the Lord in Paradise, and you would like to be certain of that, read Romans 3:23, Romans 6:23, Romans 5:8 and Romans 10:8-13. Then get alone with the Lord (or with a Christian you can trust, and with whom you would be comfortable) and tell Jesus you want Him to be your personal Savior and Lord — that you turn away from sin and want Him to give you this new birth. Then believe (Eph. 2:8,9) that He has done it, and thank Him for it. The new birth is received by faith.

If it would help you to have a model prayer to follow, pray this way:

"Heavenly Father, I want to be truly your child. I turn away from sin, darkness and death by a decision of my will. I turn toward you, toward light and life. I confess that Jesus is the Lord and I believe that you raised Him from the dead. By faith I come now, in His Name. Lord Jesus, come into my life and control it. Be my Savior and my King. Give me this new birth, quicken my spirit and indwell it with your Holy Spirit. I thank you that you are now my Savior, my Lord, and that I will never have to wonder again for I will not forsake you and your gift of everlasting life.

I pray this prayer and make this confession in the blessed Name of Jesus.

Amen"

If you have prayed this prayer, or one similar to it, just this minute or long ago, you are a child of God for He has promised that "as many (every one) as received Him, to them gave (and continues to give) He power to become the sons (and daughters) of God, even to them that believe on His Name" (John 1:12). And He has also promised that all who ask will receive (Luke 11:10), and if we come to Him, we will not be rejected: "All that the Father giveth me shall come to me; and him that cometh to me I will in no wise cast out" (John 6:37).

No matter how you may feel, your salvation is a fact; for it is not rooted in how you may feel (if it were you'd be in trouble, for there may be times when you don't "feel saved"). Your salvation is rooted in, built upon, and anchored to, the promises of God. And they never change. Halleleuia!

Now, if you have gotten your salvation settled, if you have received the new birth and resolved any doubts about it, then tell someone what you have done — tell at least one person (Matt. 10:32,33; Rom. 10:9,10); then tell others as you have the opportunity.

This is the most important issue you will ever resolve — the most important thing you will ever do. And there is actually rejoicing in Heaven over the adding of <u>your</u> name to the Lamb's Book of Life! Think of that!

Glory be to God forevermore! How wonderful and gracious He is!

# Chapter 8
# How We Receive

"... how much more shall your heavenly Father give the Holy Spirit to them that ask Him?"

(Luke 11:13)

Some of God's precious people finally see the reality of the baptism in the Holy Spirit, see that it is for God's people today, but can't believe that it is for them. "Surely", they reason, "it must be for only the 'special' Christians, or for very mature Christians in positions of leadership." Many others are robbed of the blessing by this thought: "I'll be ready to receive this baptism after I get my life cleaned up, after I break that habit, or get my thought life under control, or get victory over that sin." Oh beloved, you have it reversed! Jesus doesn't baptize mature Christians because they have gotten their lives cleaned up; it's just the opposite of that! He baptizes new, or weak, Christians with this power so that they can get their lives cleaned up, so they can go on and mature, "unto a perfect (mature, complete) man, unto the measure of the stature of the fulness of Christ" (Eph. 4:13).

Don't misunderstand, now: strong Christians and mature Christians can also receive this power. It is for all Christians. If you are an ineffective Christian it will make you more effective; if you are already an effective Christian it will make you a still-more-effective Christian. Jesus said to the 120, that nucleus of the entire Body of Christ, "Ye shall receive power, after that the Holy Ghost is come upon you: and ye shall be witnesses unto me." What? Weren't they already witnesses unto Him? They had performed miracles in His Name! Of course they had already been witnesses unto

Him, but He knew much more was needed, much more would be required. So He gave them much more power for the job ahead.

But the New Testament pattern seems to say to us that the Lord's intention was that it be granted to the new Christians so they could become strong and stable, and to the unfruitful Christians so they could become fruitful. Saul was a new believer. All those people in Samaria were new believers, snatched straight out of pagan worship and the darkness of the occult. In the household of Cornelius, some of them on whom Jesus poured out His Spirit must have been children, just old enough to understand and receive the Word; all had been Christians only a few seconds, or at most a few minutes (Acts 10:2,33,44). And at Ephesus, those young Christians didn't even know there was such a Person as the Holy Ghost!

So what's different about you?

**No One Was Left Out**

It is interesting and, I believe, significant that in each instance in the Bible record of God's pouring out of His Spirit, all who were present received. At any rate, if there were any left out, any omitted and disappointed, there is no record of it. On the day of Pentecost "they were all filled with the Holy Ghost, and began to speak with other tongues, as the

Spirit gave them utterance" (Acts 2:4). In Samaria, Peter and John laid "their hands on them, and they received the Holy Ghost" (Acts 8:17); if any were excluded there is no indication of it. Saul was only one man to whom Ananias was sent, but he did receive; and one out of one is 100% (Acts 9:17,18). At Caesarea, in the house of Cornelius, "the Holy Ghost fell on all them which heard the Word" (Acts 10:44). And at Ephesus, after Paul got things straightened out, "the Holy Ghost came on them; and they (all) spake with tongues and prophesied. And all the men were about twelve" (Acts 19:6,7).

**All You Have to Do Is Ask**

If you are a born-again child of God then all you have to do to receive the baptism in the Holy Spirit is to ask. Many will say, "Oh, it can't be that simple. Surely there must be something more I must do." No, there isn't anything else to do; it really is that simple. In Luke chapter 11 Jesus gives his familiar teaching about "Ask, Seek and Knock" (Luke 11:9-12). At the conclusion of the teaching He said, "If ye then, being evil, know how to give good gifts unto your children: how much more shall your heavenly Father give the Holy Spirit to them that ask him?" (Luke 11:13). This wonderful declaration from the lips of the Master tells us two things: first, it tells us that we must <u>ask</u> or earnestly desire it (He will never override your will, not even to bless you); second, it tells us that when we ask we will receive, assuming of course that we ask in faith (James 1:6,7). Those who hunger and thirst for Him <u>shall</u> be filled (Matt. 5:6). It's plain enough; we must seek, and when we ask in faith He acts, for He is more ready to give it than we are ready to ask. He is <u>much more</u> ready to give us good gifts than we are ready to give things to our earthly children that will bless them (Luke 11:13). He is, after all, perfect. We aren't. Keep that in mind.

**What About Laying-On Of Hands?**

We are <u>so</u> inclined to want to make neat, inflexible rules. Because of this, it is often asked "but don't I have to have hands laid on me?"; or "how can this be, when there are no apostles around anymore to lay their hands on me?".

How wonderful that God is so flexible, refusing to be limited by our doctrines. Notice that at Pentecost (Acts 2:1-4) and the house of Cornelius (Acts 10:44-46) there was no laying-on of hands, while at Samaria (Acts 8:17) and Ephesus (Acts 19:6), and in the case of Saul of Tarsus (Acts 9:17) there was. Notice also that at Samaria and Ephesus the laying-on of hands was by those with apostolic authority (Peter, James, Paul); yet in the case of Saul of

Tarsus, Ananias was an utterly obscure Damascene believer, never mentioned in the Bible before, and never heard of again.

It may help you to release your faith to have hands laid on you; at times it seems that God specially anoints certain believers to lay hands on seekers to assist them. But the scriptural record tells us clearly that God is entirely free in this matter. I have seen Jesus baptize people in His Spirit under water (while they were being baptized in water) and in other remarkable circumstances. People receive in their sleep, while flying jets at 30,000 feet, walking alone, and in the chaos of rush hour traffic. While I was in a military hosptial, a nurse came in to see me about something entirely different, and ended by asking me to pray for her sister. As I did, she (the nurse) was baptized in the Holy Spirit, struck by the lightning of Jesus, and He filled her hungry heart to overflowing. Neither of us could have been more surprised. God will not be packaged, nor will He be limited by our rules.

### It Helps to Be a Child

Jesus is an expert baptizer in the Holy Spirit. He has done it millions of times, and He always does it perfectly. The problem is that we are all amateur receivers. At the time of receiving we've never done it before — not even once.

It has been my joy to watch Jesus baptize a great many people in the Holy Spirit — many hundreds of them. If I don't qualify as an "expert", at least I qualify as a "veteran"; and I have noticed a really interesting thing. I have observed two groups of people who readily and freely receive what Jesus is so freely giving them: (1) children and (2) grown-ups who have never been to church. You see, those adults who have never been to church have never been taught that it is not for our day, or that it is a work of the devil, or that it is only for ignorant mountaineers who handle rattlesnakes. They have no negative conditioning to overcome. In this way, they are "as little children"; and I understand, better and better, why Jesus was always talking about children and telling sophisticated grown-ups that they must turn "and become as little children" (Matt 18:3). Little children trust naturally and receive freely; they don't allow pride or fear to stand in the way of a blessing.

One Christian lady I knew came into this knowledge and entered into the joy of the Spirit-filled life, sharing and praying daily with her small daughter. The little girl talked of Jesus, talked to Jesus and obviously loved Him. Then the mother began to suspect that this little girl had been baptized in the Holy Spirit because she would go around the house in her daily, little-girl affairs, talking to Jesus and singing to Jesus in words that her mother could not understand. "So young," her mother thought, "Can this be real?" Finally the little girl, sensing her mother's anxiety, said to her "It's alright Mommy — it's just God talk." Last time I heard, she was still praying and singing at times in her "God talk" and growing into a strong and healthy little Christian. It helps to be a little child.

But, since so many of us fall into that very large group in the middle — adults who <u>have</u> been to church — don't be surprised or discouraged if it takes the Lord a little time to get you completely free. You may have some fears, prejudices, and false teachings to overcome. But you can. And you will. He cannot fail; therefore <u>you</u> cannot, if you will yield to Him and trust Him completely.

We only need to ask Him; and then, like a child, let Him have His way. It's really that simple.

# Chapter 9
# But What About Tongues?

"These signs shall follow them that believe .
. . they shall speak with new tongues."
(Mark 16:17)

We knew we'd get to this sooner or later,
didn't we? I believe the tongues phenomenon

is the most misunderstood, and therefore the most feared of all the blessings of God. It also has been my observation, somewhat puzzling, that those who never practice or experience this miracle talk about it most; while those who have experienced it for years seldom want to talk about it at all, unless asked a question about it.

Before we go any farther, let me make one thing clear: the baptism by Jesus in the Holy Spirit is not speaking in tongues. The baptism in the Holy Spirit is an enduement with power from on high, so that we may be fully effective, living witnesses to a fully effective, living Jesus. The baptism in the Spirit is not tongues, it is power. Never lose sight of that. However, along with the enduement with power there comes this wonderful, supernatural ability to pray in a language we have never learned. This ability is not the baptism, but it is a wonderful, extremely important blessing that seems to come as part of the package. If you want it.

### Back to the New Testament Record

There are five accounts in the New Testament of Christians receiving the gift of the Holy Spirit. In three it plainly says that, as a result of receiving this baptism, they spoke with tongues as the Spirit gave them utterance (gave them the words to speak). In the fourth, that of Saul (Paul), it is not stated that he spoke in tongues when receiving, but he later wrote about himself that he spoke with tongues more than all the Corinthians — and apparently that was a lot (I Cor. 14:18)! So if he didn't speak in tongues when he received, he certainly began at some point down the line. In the fifth description, that of the revival in Samaria, the Bible doesn't say they spoke with tongues, but it is strongly inferred. Whatever they did when Peter and John laid their hands on them, it was something so remarkable, so clearly supernatural that Simon the Sorcerer offered to pay a lot of money to be able to lay hands on people and cause them to do it. When Peter rejected Simon's offer, he told him "thou hast neither part nor lot in this matter" (Acts 8:21). The Greek word translated "matter" is "logos" which can also be translated "speaking," so Peter may have said "thou hast neither part nor lot in this speaking." Be that as it may (and there is other evidence to indicate that the Samaritan converts spoke in tongues) we can definitely say that in the New Testament Church the norm seems to have been that people receiving this baptism would speak in tongues. They may also prophesy, or magnify (praise and worship) God; there may or may not be the sound of rushing wind, or the appearance of fire, but the one thing that seems to have been more or less constant was tongues. Notice carefully that the one thing that convinced those Jewish Christians accompanying Peter ("they of the circumcision which believed") that the gentiles in Cornelius' house really had received the gift of the Holy Spirit, just the same as they had, was that "they heard them speak with tongues and magnify God" (Acts 10:45-47).

Don't put it down. We must not over-emphasize the importance of praying and praising the Lord in unknown tongues, but neither should we minimize its importance or apologize for it. Balance is often hard to find, but always worth the effort.

### Do We Have To?

I am often asked the question: "Do I have to speak in tongues to receive the baptism in the Holy Spirit?" My answer is, "No — you don't have to; you get to."

If God will not force you to be born again, He certainly won't force you to speak in tongues. I believe the clear teaching of scripture is that when you ask Jesus to baptize you in His Holy Spirit, He does it — whether you speak in tongues, prophesy, see a vision, have a good feeling, have a bad feeling or have nothing seem to happen. By faith, just because you sincerely ask, He does it. Receive it, claim it as your own and act on it. Don't let anyone talk you out of it.

But — and this is a very important "but" — it seems to have been the New Testament norm, the plan of God if you will, that they began to pray and magnify the Lord in other tongues at the time of receiving this baptism. And, although it is not scripture, St. Augustine is recorded as having said in the 6th century "We still do what the apostles did when they laid hands on the Samaritans and called down the Holy Spirit on them by laying on of hands. It is expected that converts should speak with new tongues."*

It has been my observation, over a period of 10 very active years, that those who have received the baptism in the Holy Spirit but do not pray in tongues are never really satisfied and, significantly, never fully released in the supernatural gifts of the Spirit (I Cor. 12:7-10). I do not "promote speaking in tongues"; I never have, and never intend to. But I am more and more convinced that there is something extremely important, something almost pivotal about opening your mouth in faith, trusting Jesus to give you bread and not a stone, trusting Him to give you a fish and not a serpent, speaking words your mind does not comprehend. Believe the promise that the Spirit

---

*Lindsay, Gordon: 30 Objections to Speaking in Other Tongues, and the Bible Answer, Christ for the Nations (Dallas, Texas, 1968)

is making "intercession for the saints according to the will of God" (Rom. 8:27). It is a faith act. Every time you do it you are out on the water, being built up "on your most Holy faith, praying in the Holy Ghost" (Jude 20).*

We'll come back to this, but remember that it is an act of faith and it is entirely voluntary.

## It is Strictly Up to You

Some fear this experience because they think they will be overwhelmed by an unseen force and be "out of control", caught up in some sort of irresistable spell of ecstasy. Nothing could be further from the truth. If we had no control, no choice about speaking or not speaking, then all those instructions in I Corinthians 14 about when to speak, when not to speak, etc. would be absurd and unnecessary. They aren't. The Word of God is neither absurd nor unnecessary — not one word of it. Be assured: all utterances in tongues, whether prayer in the Spirit, singing in the Spirit, or a message in tongues for the church, are completely voluntary. Most are not accompanied by any "feeling" at all. The good feelings are nice — I love them — but they are neither essential nor inevitable. If you seek them you may be disappointed; if you fear them you will be delightfully surprised.

*For another thought along this line, see Chapter 10, "A Step Across the Line", page 107.

82

**It Is Only Prayer**

When I received this baptism I was 40 years old, had a wife and four children, three university degrees, had served as a Marine Corps infantry officer in Korea and Vietnam, and had been over much of the world; yet I was so hungry and thirsty for the newly-discovered reality of God that in many ways I was like a child. I had no books, no tapes, no teachers, no prayer group — only my Bible, my needs and the Lord. There was so much I didn't know, but I was sure of this much: I had discovered that Jesus is real, "a very present help" (Ps. 46:1), and I both needed and wanted everything He would do in my life.

Because this new language came to me with the baptism in the Holy Spirit, I thought I had received "the gift of tongues." I was delighted! As time went by I found fellowship; one night I received an anointing and nervously spoke a short little word of prophecy. Within myself I thought "Praise the Lord! I have the gift of prophecy!" Then, a little later, I prayed for a very sick woman and she was instantly healed. I thought "Glory to God! Now I have the gift of healing!" It was pretty exciting and, without realizing it, within myself I was wearing these gifts like merit badges on a sash, or stars on a Holy Ghost campaign medal. You may laugh, but I just didn't know any better. I thought I "had" three gifts of the Spirit. Then one day it occurred to me that I couldn't prophesy any time I wanted to, nor could I heal sick people any time I wanted to. But I was confused, because I could speak in tongues any time I wanted to. Then, when I discovered that this utterance that came to me with the baptism in the Holy Spirit was really prayer — not the gift of tongues, but a new dimension of prayer — everything fell into place in my understanding. It was a breakthrough in terms of understanding manifestations of the Holy Spirit. Let me explain the difference.

## Praying in Tongues or the Gift of Tongues?

**1. Praying in Tongues.** Praying in tongues (I Cor. 14:14) is prayer in a language you never learned, one unknown to your mind. It may be French, Russian, Navajo, Swahili or any other language. But it is a language. Remember that on the day of Pentecost the Christians were praising God in at least sixteen known languages, real languages, understood by those world-traveling Jews who heard them (Acts 2:4-11).

**a. I Have Seen and Heard the Miracle.** I have twice ministered the baptism in the Holy Spirit to individuals who began to pray in Latin. They didn't realize it, neither was educated, neither knew a single word of Latin. But I knew enough to understand most of what they were saying, and they were praising God. I remember others who prayed in Spanish and French. On one ministry tour in Haiti I heard a young Haitian man praising God in eloquent, flawless English. Of course there are English-speaking Christians in Haiti, but this caught my attention because it was so perfect and without any accent. I asked a Haitian next to me what he was doing, and she answered, "Those people are speaking in tongues." Then I asked the man, in English, if he spoke English and he only looked embarassed and confused. I asked again and he became even more embarassed and confused but didn't reply. Then I asked him in French if he spoke or understood English and he answered in French that he did not. I then confirmed this with his pastor: he knew not a word of English. He was praising God in tongues, in that case English, a language unknown to him.

At a conference in St. Louis a group of Christians was seeking the baptism in the Spirit and George Otis was praying for them. He had prayed for them in English and had begun quietly to pray over the group in tongues. A young man from India walked in, listened and spoke out: "Someone in here is speaking Hindi with mixed Sanskrit and that is my native tongue! Who is it?" Of course no one knew, so he went around the room, listening, and discovered that it was George. When I asked the young Indian what it was that George was saying in Hindi with mixed Sanskrit, he told me that he was praising and thanking God, and then he asked God to send down His Spirit to touch and bless those people! Glory to God! That's exciting!

Another Bible teacher I know, while preaching among Mexicans, ministered the baptism in the Spirit to a girl who spoke no English and she recited the 23rd Psalm in perfect English! I could fill this entire book with such examples from real experience, but of course that would be a mistake.

There are so many hundreds of languages in the world (more than 23 separate languages spoken among the Maya Indians alone) and some of them won't even sound like real languages to your ear; but every utterance will be a language with meaning (I Cor. 14:10). Some believe that we may, in addition, speak in angelic tongues from time to time because of Paul's statement in I Corinthians 13:1, "Though I speak with the tongues of men and of angels . . .". Perhaps we do; I don't know.

This prayer (or praise) is offered by the individual believer, normally in private, and needs no interpretation for God understands. The direction of travel is up — from the Christian to the Lord. And it is voluntary, strictly under your control; you can do it anytime you choose (I Cor. 14:15).

**b. And It Is Perfect Prayer.** People often ask me "What good does it do to pray in tongues when you don't even know what you are saying?" My reply is that it is important that we not know what we're saying because this way we can't mess it up! You see, it is God's perfect provision for us to be able to pray perfect prayer and offer perfect praise. The reason that it is perfect is that God gives us every word (I Cor. 14:14; Romans 8:26,27). When we intercede, it is perfect intercession, even when we don't know anything about the problem.

It is not possible to pray an unscriptural prayer in tongues, for God is not confused. It is not possible to pray a selfish prayer in tongues. It is not possible to pray an unwise or ineffective prayer in tongues. Don't you see the importance of that?

. The same thing applies to praise and worship. With our understanding (native language) we probably have a praise vocabulary of only 20 or 25 words. But in the Spirit, we have potentially the praise vocabularies of all the languages in all the Universe. Have you ever wished you had words to express how wonderful the Lord is and how much you love and appreciate Him? This way you can do it — without limitation. You can express the inexpressible!

That's why Paul decided, after sorting it all out, "What is it then? I will pray with the spirit, and I will pray with the understanding also: I will sing with the spirit, and I will sing with the understanding also" (I Cor. 14:15). He says here

# The gift of tongues vs. praying in Spirit.

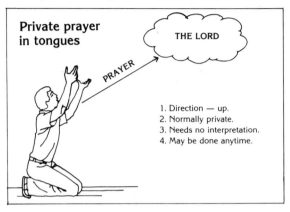

**Private prayer in tongues**

THE LORD

PRAYER

1. Direction — up.
2. Normally private.
3. Needs no interpretation.
4. May be done anytime.

**The gift of tongues**

THE LORD

THE MESSAGE

THE MESSAGE    THE CHURCH

1. Direction — down.
2. Normally public.
3. Must be interpreted.
4. Can only be done when there is anointing and only by the one the Spirit selects.

that his prayer life was not complete until he prayed both ways — naturally and super-naturally. And he says that his praise was not complete until he worshipped and sang songs of praise to the Lord in both ways. Neither is an adequate substitute for the other.

2. **The Gift of Tongues.** The gift of tongues (I Cor. 12:10) is <u>also</u> an utterance in a language unknown to the speaker, but here the similarity in function ends. This gift is from the Lord, to the Church assembled, and <u>must</u> be interpreted (I Cor. 14:5) or it does no <u>good.</u> In fact, such public utterance without interpretation can do harm (I Cor. 14:6-13). Note that the direction of travel is <u>down</u> in this case — from the Lord to the church. This is <u>also</u> voluntary, in that we may refuse to speak (I Cor. 14:27,28,32); but we can only manifest this gift when given a momentary anointing — not when we choose, but when the Spirit chooses (I Cor. 12:8-11).

## But Wait a Minute

You may be remembering that in I Corinthians 12:30 Paul asked the rhetorical question "Do all speak with tongues?" and the answer is obviously "no". Doesn't this mean that only certain people will speak or pray in tongues? No, it doesn't mean that. Notice that the same Paul, under the same anointing, in the same letter to the same church, wrote in chapter 14 and verse 5 "I would (it is my desire and intention) that ye all spake with tongues." Now, on its face that seems like a contradiction; but of course it is not. God is not confused. If you will study chapters 12, 13 and 14 together (and that's the way they should be studied — they are a trilogy) you will see that what's being discussed in the latter part of chapter 12 (verses 28-30) is the question of ministries performed in the church, not private worship. Then you will see that what is being discussed in chapter 14 is private worship and prayer, and individual behavior in church in the occasional manifestations of speaking or praying in tongues, along with prophecy and other manifestations of the Spirit. For an excellent example of this compare chapter 12, verse 29 ("are all prophets?") with chapter 14, verse 31 ("Ye may all prophesy"). You see, not all will be called to the ministry of a prophet, but all may (occasionally) prophesy in church. Not all will be called to a ministry of speaking messages in tongues to the church, but all are expected to speak or pray in tongues privately as individuals, and to occasionally speak a message in tongues in public church meetings when (and if) the Holy Spirit chooses.

You may be surprised to learn that praying

in tongues is dealt with in other parts of the New Testament also (such as Jude 20), and in one such passage we are apparently even <u>directed</u> to pray this way (Eph. 6:17,18).

It is a work of the Lord; it is a wonderful, life-changing blessing. And it is for you.

# Chapter 10
# There Are Obstacles In Your Path

"Be not overcome of (by) evil, but (rather) overcome evil with good."

(Romans 12:21)

I am convinced that when a Christian asks Jesus to baptize him in the Holy Spirit he receives (Luke 11:13). By faith it is done and we should count it done, for God is faithful to His word (Ps. 138:2; Titus 1:2).

But I have learned that there are some hindrances which will interfere with our being able freely to receive what Jesus is freely giving us. You might call them obstacles, or stumbling blocks; and they need to be dealt with, in advance, or you may be frustrated and hindered in receiving.

These hindrances are: unforgiveness, occult sin, the sins of our ancestors and the failure to understand how to respond to what Jesus is doing. A thorough discussion of these is beyond the scope of this book, but we need to know enough to be able to eliminate them as obstacles to our receiving. I don't want you frustrated, and neither does the Lord.

### We Must Forgive

A common obstacle to receiving anything from God, other than salvation, is unforgiveness. It will usually be found operating with its partner, resentment. Jesus said, in the sermon on the mount, "for if ye forgive men their trespasses, your Heavenly Father will also forgive you: but if ye forgive not men their trespasses, neither will your Father forgive your trespasses" (Matt. 6:14,15). Then, in His great teaching on forgiveness, Jesus said that if we do not forgive, the Heavenly Father will deliver us up to "the tormentors" (Matt. 18:21-35). Furthermore, in His teaching on the prayer of faith, He said, "And when ye stand praying, forgive, if ye have aught against any" (Mk. 11:25) which infers very strongly that if we don't forgive we may as well not pray. Finally, in Ephesians 4:32 we are commanded to forgive: "And be ye kind one to another, tenderhearted, forgiving one another, even as God for Christ's sake hath forgiven you."

This can be summarized, then, by saying the Bible gives these reasons that we must forgive:

a. In order to be forgiven
b. In order to be free of torment
c. In order for our prayers to be heard
d. It is a commandment.

Isn't that enough?

**But How Can We Forgive?** The way we forgive is just to forgive. Now, it won't help you a bit to tell you that if I don't explain. Forgiving is easy once you understand; and in order to understand you must realize the following facts about forgiveness:

**(1) They don't have to deserve it.** Most people whom you need to forgive are guilty — no doubt about it — and do not deserve your forgiveness. They may not even want it. But that has nothing to do with forgiving them. Jesus has forgiven you, not because you deserved it but because you needed it. And He

95

has told us "freely ye have received, freely give." Vengeance is the Lord's, and He will repay (Hebr. 10:30). Don't wait for them to deserve your forgiveness; they probably never will.

(2) **Forgiveness begins as a decision — not an emotion.** You don't have to feel all gooshy inside in order to forgive. In fact, you may be filled with ugly emotions at the very thought of the person(s). But you can forgive — right now — by a deliberate act of your will. Once the decision is made, and the forgiveness spoken in prayer, then somewhere down the road a release will come and your emotions will catch up with your decision. Please note: it may not be necessary to tell the people that you forgive them (I don't advise it unless you feel the Lord is telling you to do it); but you must tell the Lord. If the Lord should require you to tell them, and if they don't accept your forgiveness, that's their problem. You will be free.

(3) **Resentment and unforgiveness don't hurt the resentee; but they will poison, injure and kill the resentor.** I have discovered from time to time that there are people who resented me whom I had never even met! It didn't hurt me at all, but it was consuming them and robbing them of their peace. A lady I didn't know called me once from another state and said that she needed a miracle in her life

and wanted me to pray for her. But first, she said, she needed my forgiveness. I said, "How could you need my forgiveness? I don't even know you." She said that another Christian had told her I was a bad person, teaching false doctrine, and that she had believed him, resented me, and repeated his story to others. It had cost her her peace and was standing in the way of the miracle she needed. It wasn't hurting me, but it was surely hurting her.

(4) **No one is excluded.** I have been amazed to learn how many Christians resent God. It seems that most don't want to admit it because to the traditional Christian mind it is rather unthinkable, so they keep it within themselves as a dark and private secret, yet wondering at times if they will be struck with lightning. Listen, if you feel that way, deal with it! Forgive Him — He knows how you feel anyway. If it's a person who has hurt you, and that person is dead, we still must forgive him. Of course, we cannot speak the forgiveness to those who have died, but that is usually not necessary (or desirable) anyway. The key fact is that the forgiveness must be spoken to God and the resentment released — that's how the freedom comes. The fact that the resented one is dead makes no difference at all.

(5) **You must forgive yourself.** Another one often omitted in forgiveness prayers is yourself. You can't get away with that — you

<u>must</u> forgive yourself. Most Christians, at first thought, feel that it is presumptuous to forgive yourself — that only God or other people can forgive you. But that's not so. God has forgiven you (if you have asked Him to), and forgotten. But the devil remembers, and loves to accuse you. To withhold forgiveness from yourself is to put yourself in agreement with the devil and at cross purposes with the work and will of God. You must forgive yourself also. Here many will say, "But I don't deserve it!" Of course you don't deserve it; that has nothing to do with it. You don't deserve God's forgiveness either; He gives it because you need it. You must forgive yourself, as surely as you must forgive others.

## Occult Sin and False Religions

Occult sin is a large and difficult-to-define category of sin. The word "occult" means "hidden" and a great deal of occult activity has to do with seeking hidden knowledge or information outside of scriptural guidelines. Included are all forms of divination (fortune telling, palm-reading, crystal balls, ouija boards, water witching, etc.), magic, witchcraft, astrology and horoscopes, superstitions, ESP, psychic phenomena, spiritism, hypnotism, levitation and all related activities.

All these are strictly forbidden by the Word of God, both Old Testament and New. He considers all such activities spiritual adultery ("whoring after other Gods") and has never changed His mind about it because He knows it will poison and eventually destroy us. The primary scriptural basis for what I have just said is found in Deuteronomy 18:9-14. False religions and occult philosophies cannot be separated from occult sin because most false religions and philosophies involve occult activity. And all involve seeking after supernatural guidance, comfort or power from a source other than the Holy Spirit of God. They deny the Word of God and there is therefore no light (truth) in them (Is. 8:19,20). They are an abomination to the Lord, and they give the devil a legal right to hinder you, injure you and keep you out of God's blessings (Is 59:1,2).

Almost everyone has been touched in some way by occult sin. Virtually all newspapers and magazines contain horoscope readings. Fortune telling and magic are part of most public school festivals (and, sad to relate, many church activities). Hypnotism (the modern name for what the Bible calls "enchantment") is a common form of entertainment and is taught to many in the health professions. Se'ances (calling up spirits) are a common feature of young girls' slumber parties (while slumber seldom is). If you have never been involved in any of these activities you are most unusual, and should be grateful.

At this point many will say "but I didn't take it seriously" or "I only read the horoscopes to see how silly they were" or "I only went to the fortuneteller for laughs." It doesn't seem to matter whether we take it seriously or not; God takes it seriously ("For all that do these things are an abomination unto the Lord: . . ." Deut. 18:12) and the devil takes it seriously. Satan is a legal expert, knows his rights and will take advantage of every opportunity we give him to injure us because he hates us. I could cite many examples, both in scripture and from personal experience, but space does not permit. In addition to all this, we are told to avoid even the appearance of evil (I Thes. 5:22). The Word of God leaves us no room even to dabble in the occult — not in any way.

People often say to me "But that is only harmless fun." My reply is, "It may be fun, but it isn't harmless." It is deadly.

**What Must We Do?** To be free from all hindrance due to occult involvement, whether deliberate or innocent, whether we remember it or not, we must renounce* it in prayer and call upon the Lord to deliver us from all bondage that has come into our lives because of it. He will do just that.

*To renounce simply means to take a stand against something, to disown, to reject, and to state your opposition to it. In this case the renunciation takes the form of a prayer.

It is probably obvious to you, but inherent in renouncing occult sin is turning away (repenting) from it. You must turn from all occult practices and rid yourself of occult books and materials; it is scriptural to burn them (Acts 19:18-20).

Some will say "but all that was forgiven and washed away when I came to the Lord"; but I'm not talking about the forgiveness of the sin, I'm talking about trouble that came in (fear, doubt, confusion, compulsion, etc.) because of the sin. Perhaps the sin was forgiven years ago — there may still be resultant trouble that has not been dealt with. If there is, deal with it. The Lord wants you free.

## The Sins of Your Ancestors

Have you ever noticed that certain types of problems tend to run in families? Depression tends to run in families; so do suicide, alcoholism, adultery and divorce, child-abuse, fears, occult powers, violent anger, incest and a great many other forms of trouble. This has been commonly observed to be true, but no one has been able adequately to explain it. Environmental influence has been suggested in sociological studies. Biologists have searched without success for genes which would explain such behavior. Psychiatrists have suggested conditioning, rebellion and projection of emotions as causes, but clear evidence is lacking.

No one seems really to know. But I believe at least part of the explanation can be found in God's word, starting with the first Commandment, ". . . for I the Lord thy God am a jealous God, visiting the iniquity of the fathers upon the children unto the third and fourth generation . . ." (Ex. 20:5).

The context of the First Commandment is idolatry — the following of the occult practices, the pagan gods and their witch-doctor priests, sorcerers and astrologers, which prevailed in pagan societies.

Read the challenge God hurled at Babylon through the prophet Isaiah: "Stand now with thine enchantments, and with the multitude of thy sorceries, . . . Let now the astrologers, the stargazers, the monthly prognosticators, stand up, and save thee . . . Behold, they shall be as stubble; . . . they shall not deliver (even) themselves . . ." (Is. 47:12-14). God told them (verses 9 and 10) that this judgement was coming upon them because they had trusted in their sorceries and enchantments. You see, what we put our trust in, in the Lord's eyes, is our god. I'll say that again: what we put our trust in, in the Lord's eyes, is our god. Think on that.

Perhaps your grandmother was a fortuneteller, or your great-grandfather was a water witch. Perhaps your father, grandfather, an aunt or an uncle was a student of the pagan mysteries of Egypt or Greece, devoted to secret societies which deny Jesus as the only savior. Perhaps there was one in your ancestry given to some prevailing dark sin. You may not even know about it; still the trouble may come — the curse may persist, relentlessly plaguing innocent offspring because the door was opened back there somewhere in past generations.

Does this seem unfair? I won't defend God — He doesn't need me to defend Him. But it does occur to me that He had it all written in a Book thousands of years ago, at an enormous cost in the blood of martyrs, and He expects us to read it.

Now, I realize that each of us is responsible for his own sin, his own salvation, and that we must come to God for ourselves to be forgiven and saved (Ezek. 18). But I'm not talking about being saved or lost, I'm not talking about inheriting life or death. I'm talking about trouble.

There are many more passages of scripture to establish this, but for our present purposes let it suffice to say that if there is even a chance that there is some sort of limitation hindering you, some sort of curse passed down from past generations, the only sensible thing to do is to take it to the Lord. The good news is that if there is any such hindrance in your life, even something you don't understand, or for causes you have no knowledge of, God will set you free! He understands and He knows all about it. All you have to do is ask (Joel 2:32). And if there is no such problem, no such curse in your ancestry, it never hurts us to pray. Why take a chance?

This one simple prayer may change your life; and, once prayed, it never needs to be repeated. It lasts a lifetime! Pray once, count it done, thank Him for your freedom and leave it behind.

**You Must Do the Praying**

The final obstacle to clear away is merely the failure to understand something. And it is so simple, yet it keeps many hungry Christians from freely receiving the baptism in the Holy Spirit and enjoying its benefits.

The simple fact, missed by so many, is this: the Holy Spirit doesn't pray, or speak, in tongues — Christians do. That's all there is to it, but failure to understand this creates problems in some people's lives. Let me show you why.

Some Christians, especially those with backgrounds in the pentecostal denominations, believe that the Holy Spirit will possess them somehow, move their tongues, chins, lips, diaphragms and force them to speak in tongues. Many are "experience"-oriented, and have been led to believe — sincerely — that if they receive this blessing they will have a powerful, perhaps overwhelming emotional/spiritual experience and be virtually compelled to speak in tongues. Many are taught to "tarry," or wait for the Lord to do this to them. I have seen them pray sincerely "Lord — baptize me in the Holy Ghost!", then kneel or stand there, hands lifted to Heaven, mouths open, eyes closed, with nothing seeming to happen. It gets awkward; it gets painful; it's unnecessary.

They are waiting for Jesus to do what He is waiting for <u>them</u> to do. To speak.

Beloved seeker after God, don't you see why nothing seems to happen in such a situation? I have personally prayed for one who had "tarried" for 40 years! And I have prayed for several who had been waiting at that impasse for 25 years or more. They wanted it so badly, and went through all kinds of self-examination, guilt, frustration and even resentment of God, because they couldn't seem to receive. They thought God was withholding the blessing from them for some reason. These all received immediately — without exception — once they understood. They could have had it in 40 seconds instead of 40 years. What a loss — both to them and to the Kingdom.

On the day of Pentecost "they were all filled with the Holy Ghost, and (they) began to speak with other tongues as the Spirit gave them utterance (gave them words to speak)."

Who spoke? They spoke. At the house of Cornelius "they heard them (those who were receiving) speak with tongues." Who was speaking? Them. At Ephesus "they spake with tongues and prophesied." Who spake? They did. When Paul wrote his letter to the church at Corinth, he said "I thank my God I speak with tongues." Who spoke? He did.

Now, I realize that each of us is unique. No two of us are alike, and no two of us will have exactly the same experience of God. Some have a dramatic experience of conversion, or the new birth; others have no "experience" at all. God, recognizing our uniqueness, does a custom job on each of us. And one of the things I appreciate about Him is that He is very gentle.

In the initial praying or speaking in tongues some of us have a very powerful experience; others of us do not. For some the initial utterance comes easily — almost irresistably; for others this is not true. Some seem to struggle. But no matter how easy, or how awkward it may seem, one thing runs true: you do it, and you do it because you choose to do it.

So the essence of the matter is simply this: you must open your mouth and, by a deliberate act of your will, speak — not English (or any other language you have learned), for you can't speak two languages at the same time.

You must articulate sounds, syllables, words — not knowing what you are going to say. Jesus is faithful and He will see to it that what you say is real — that's the miracle in your mouth.

## A Step Across the Line

At this point I must say that for most people this is a highly significant line we step across — much more significant than many of us realize. You see, all your life (up to this moment) you have been mind-dominated. First you decided what to say, and then you said it; but there is no faith in that. Utterances in the Spirit are exactly the opposite: you must open your mouth and speak, not having the slightest idea what you are going to say until you hear yourself saying it. It is a completely irrational thing. You are acting in faith. Peter was acting in faith when he stepped out of the boat and onto the water; but if he had waited in the boat until the water got hard, he would still be in the boat. Think on that.

And the significant thing is that the Holy Spirit, through your human spirit, is now in the preeminant position over your mind (the "natural man" of I Cor. 2:14). Romans 8:14 is being fulfilled ("For as many as are led by the Spirit of God, they are the sons of God"), and you have entered into a higher, freer dimension of the Christian life. Your mind will object to this, but don't let that stop you. When you pray in tongues the prayer comes from your spirit, not from your mind (I Cor. 14:14).

So your part is to speak, and Jesus will take over there, performing the miracle. But remember this one thing: <u>You</u> must do the praying.

# Chapter 11
# Entering In

"Blessed are they which do hunger and thirst after righteousness: for they shall be filled."

(Matt. 5:6)

## The Hungry and Thirsty Are Filled

If you are sincerely hungering and thirsting for more of God then Jesus has promised that you will be filled (Matt 5:6). The indifferent and the antagonistic will probably be left alone, for Jesus is a perfect gentleman and will never intrude where He is not welcome.

Some take the attitude, "Well, I guess it's alright. If the Lord wants to give it to me, I guess He'll give it to me; but I'm in no hurry, and I'm certainly not going to seek it." They seem never to receive. Small wonder! Imagine a lost person who says, "Well, I guess this salvation is alright. If God wants to save me I guess He'll save me; but I'm in no rush, and I'm certainly not going to seek it." Do you think that person will be run down and tackled from the rear by the Holy Ghost as he walks away from God, and be forced to receive the new birth? No chance at all! It is those who hunger and thirst after Him whom He blesses — those who press through and lay hold of His garment, those who say, "Yes Lord! I want YOU! I want every good and perfect gift you have for me!" It is these whom He delights in blessing.

Do you recognize your need? Do you want Him and the perfect blessings He has prepared for you (I Cor. 2:9)? Then you shall be filled. Jesus has promised.

### "But I'm Not Worthy"

People often say to me, "I want the baptism

110

in the Holy Spirit, but I'm not worthy." My answer is, "Great! Once you realize you're not worthy, you are ready to receive!" Of course you're not worthy — nobody is! This baptism in the Holy Spirit is not a reward for exceptional performance as a Christian; it isn't the "reward of the Holy Spirit"; it is the "gift of the Holy Spirit." No one is worthy of salvation; and no one is worthy of the gift of the Holy Spirit. He gives the fulness of His Spirit to us, in spite of the fact that we don't deserve it, because He knows we need it. All the things He does for us are gracious gifts — not rewards.

### Fear Not

There are some fears that may come against you as you prepare to receive. Most common are the fear of not receiving (and being disappointed), and the fear that you will be just "making it up."

**The Fear of Not Receiving.** The answer to the fear that you will not receive is the promise of Jesus. He said, "Ask, and it shall be given unto you; . . . for everyone that asketh receiveth" (Luke 11:9,10). What could be more clear? In Acts 10:34 and Romans 2:11 it is plainly written that God is no respector of persons (plays no favorites); He blesses all with equal generosity. And in I John 5:14,15 it is written "And this is the confidence that we have in Him, that, if we ask anything according to His will, He heareth us: and if we know that He hear us, whatsoever we ask, we know that we have the petitions that we desired of Him." Do you believe that it is His will for you (and all other believers) to have this power? Then you cannot fail to receive it.

**The Fear of Making It Up.** When I first began to pray in tongues, the devil whispered to my mind, "Does that sound like a real language to you?" I replied, "No, as a matter of fact it sounds pretty weird to me." Then he planted the seed of doubt with, "Well then, what makes you think it is a real language?" (Caution: at this point he will get you out of the faith realm and into the sense realm, and there he will rob you. That is his home ballpark.) He doesn't try that with me anymore, but if he did my answer to the second question would be, "I don't think it's a real language, I know it's a real language. And the reason I know it is real is that Jesus promised that if I asked for the real thing I wouldn't get a counterfeit. He promised in Luke 11:9-13 that if I ask for bread I won't be deceived by receiving a rock in a bread wrapper. I will get the real thing! If imperfect, sinful, earthly fathers wouldn't pull such a deception on their children, how much more can we trust our heavenly father to give us valid, perfect spiritual gifts?

One night I prayed with a lady who

received the baptism in the Spirit and she began to pray in a <u>strange</u> sounding tongue that sounded to me more like chickens clucking than a real language. I didn't want to undermine her confidence so I didn't say anything about it; but within myself I said, "Lord — I've heard a lot of strange languages in my time, but I don't believe that one — that's just too weird." I said, "Really Lord — after all — there <u>is</u> a limit."

The very next morning I was at a nearby military base waiting for my family. My legs were hurting and I needed to sit down. The <u>only</u> seat was next to two oriental men (they appeared to be Indochinese) and they were carrying on an animated conversation in that <u>very same</u> "chicken clucking!" I said, "Father, forgive me. I get the message — I'll never doubt again, no matter how strange some languages may seem to my mind." I have heard tonal languages in Vietnam; I have heard one spoken by Central American Indians that sounds like birds chirping. I no longer doubt <u>anything</u> that is spoken in a scriptural context.

**What About Wrong (Evil) Spirits?** I hate even to mention this, but I suppose I must: it is clear that we need never fear that we may ask for the Holy Spirit and receive, instead, some unholy spirit (Lk 11:9-13). There is not one line of scripture to suggest that; in fact, the entire

Bible declares just the opposite! Yet many sincere seekers after the things of God have been put in bondage of fear by such irresponsible teaching and preaching. They have been told not to ask for the Holy Spirit because they may, instead, be invaded by some evil spirit. How terrible! How sad. If this were a valid danger then it would not be safe to seek salvation, for you might ask Jesus to come into your heart and, instead, have the devil come into your heart. How absurd! How tragic that such a thing is even considered! Dear hungry one, there is no reason even to entertain such a thought. Jesus promised that those who hunger and thirst after righteousness shall be filled with the blessings of God (Matt. 5:6) — not the curses of the devil. Press on into the good things of God; draw with joy from the wells of salvation! If you are thirsty, Jesus is saying to you, "Come and drink" (Is. 12:3; Jn. 7:37).

Incidentally, I love the fact that Jesus also said that if we ask for a fish (oldest symbol of the things of the Lord) we needn't fear receiving instead a serpent (you know who that represents). This is certainly not a major revelation, but I think it is a nice reminder for those who have ears to hear. He is so very thoughtful.

**Let Me Reassure You.** I have become convinced that it is not possible to "make it up." I

114

believe now that if you ask Jesus in faith for this heavenly language of prayer, and trust Him enough to begin to speak, not knowing what you are saying, <u>He</u> will <u>see to it</u> that what comes out of your mouth is real and perfect (after all — <u>you</u> certainly can't). Your part is to speak — <u>His</u> part is to work the miracle, causing it to be a real language. Therefore I don't believe it is <u>possible</u> to "make it up." Let me give you a real-life illustration.

This really happened — a wonderful story. A young man in a pentecostal denomination had been seeking this baptism, not knowing what you now know. At every service, every altar call, he was a seeker, yet never seemed to receive. He just kept "tarrying." Finally, one Sunday night, he answered the invitation as usual. (By this time nobody paid much attention . . . he always did that.) After kneeling a while, he stood up, turned around, lifted his hands and began to speak some strange words. The people rejoiced! They all said, "Praise the Lord! Brother so-and-so finally got it!" The young man let them rejoice a few minutes and then said, "I hate to disappoint you, but I have to confess. I made all that up — that wasn't tongues, I just thought I'd see if I could fool you." And then he hung his head, feeling worse than ever. Then a young Chinese exchange student in the first pew said, "Brother, would you like to know <u>what</u> you

115

just made up?" The young seeker, puzzled, said he would. Then the Chinese brother said, "You just prayed a beautiful prayer in perfect Mandarin Chinese."

Do you realize the significance of this true story? That man not only thought he had "made it up" — he intended to! Yet, because he had previously asked Jesus, sincerely, for a real language, when he finally opened his mouth and spoke words he could not understand, Jesus took over and out came perfect Mandarin Chinese. And God loved that man enough to bring a Christian all the way from China to reassure him that what he had was real.

Have no fear, take no thought, just trust Jesus. He loves you and won't allow you to be hurt or deceived.

### Clearing Away the Obstacles

Before you ask Jesus to be your baptizer, it is always wise to pray the following prayers, if you have never done so: the prayer of forgiveness; the prayer of renunciation of the occult; and the prayer asking the Lord to deliver you from the sins of your ancestors.

**1. The Prayer of Forgiveness.** The need for forgiving was explained in Chapter 10. If you have never prayed such a prayer, pray as follows:

"Heavenly Father, I thank you that you

have forgiven me, every time I have asked you, not because I deserve it but because I need it. Therefore I do forgive everyone who ever hurt me, abused me, used me, failed to understand or appreciate me, or for any other reason caused me to resent them. I forgive them all, in Jesus' name, not because they deserve it, but because I want to be free and because I want to obey you. I ask you to forgive me for the resentment I have held, and I thank you that I am forgiven."

(There are almost always some that the Lord wants you to forgive by name — ask Him to show you who they are, and then pray the following:)

"In the name of Jesus I specifically forgive _____ ."

(You speak their names — each one — and release their guilt to the Lord.)

"And in the name of Jesus I forgive myself; and as I do Lord, I set myself in agreement with you, and against the devil. For you have forgiven me and you have forgotten. Therefore I forgive myself and I ask you to help me forget. And, Father, I call upon you to deliver me from every bondage that has come into my life because of unforgiveness and resentment, and I thank you that I am free."

(Note: If you have prayed such a prayer in

117

the past, you may need to bring it up to date.)

**2. Renunciation of the Occult.** This was also explained in Chapter 10. If you have never done so, you should pray as follows:

"In the name of Jesus I renounce the devil and all his works. I renounce all things occult, the doctrine of reincarnation, every false religion, every cult, every philosophy or any other group that would deny the truth of Scriptures. I renounce every form of divination, spiritism, magic, astrology, psychic power, sorcery, enchantment and every supernatural thing that is not done in the name of Jesus, or that doesn't glorify Jesus. I further renounce everything I have read or studied concerning these things."

(At this point ask the Lord to call to your mind all such things that have touched your life and renounce them by name, whether you took them seriously or not, and pray:)

"In the name of Jesus I specifically renounce _____ and I call upon the Lord to deliver me and set me free from every bondage that may have come into my life because of these things, and I thank you that I am free."

**3. The Sins of the Ancestors.** As explained in Chapter 10, this prayer needs to be prayed only once in a lifetime. If you have never done so, pray as follows:

"Heavenly Father, in the name of Jesus I call upon you to deliver me and set me free from the consequences of the sins of my ancestors. Sever every line of demonic heredity — break every curse, every line of trouble that has come down upon me through my family. Set me completely free, now and forever, and I thank you that I <u>am</u> free."

## Get Comfortable

Since you have a choice, get yourself in a place and situation where you are comfortable. It is important, all other things being provided for, to be able to relax, be undistracted and single-minded on the Lord. After all, the baptism in the Holy Spirit is the second most important thing that will ever happen to you. And it only happens once.

It seems to be that the front of a church, or prayer meeting, or Christian conference is one of the most difficult places for most people to receive. Please don't misunderstand me; a great many people receive that way, and I thank God for it. But many find it hard to receive in such a situation because there are so many people watching, and the pressures and anxieties of all kinds are multiplied. If you have a choice, get alone, or with a trusted friend, or in a small prayer group. As we have observed already, Jesus is an expert baptizer; but we are all amateur receivers. He understands that, so make it as easy for yourself as you can.

If the Lord tells you to go and receive in front of a multitude, go there and be obedient. But if he doesn't, make yourself as comfortable as possible.

And a word of caution: don't make declarations about what you "will never do"; that thing may be exactly what God will require of you. It's alright to say, "Lord — I'd really rather not," but it's dangerous to say "I will never do it that way." I have begun to suspect that when we make such a statement, it becomes a requirement for us that we do the very thing we said we would "never" do.

Be careful, be sensible, be blessed.

## Come and Drink

On that great day of the Feast of Tabernacles Jesus stood in the street and cried out, "If any man thirst, let him come to me, and drink. He that believeth on me, as the scripture hath said, out of his belly (innermost being — the center of yourself) shall flow rivers of living water" (John 7:37,38). Then, to be certain we don't miss it, verse 39 tells us clearly that what Jesus meant by "living water" was the Holy Spirit, which would be given after He was glorified. He said all we have to do is come to

Him and drink in the Spirit of God; then, as a result, rivers of this Spirit's manifestations will flow out of us to bless God and touch the lives of others. We drink, He fills us, and we overflow with praise, prayer and other blessings of the Spirit. But there seems to be a problem . . .

## How Can You Drink a Spirit?

The Greek word translated "Spirit" in your Bible is "pneuma" which means spirit, breath, air or wind. From this Greek word we derive such English words as pneumonia and pneumatic. So, in one very real sense, the Holy Spirit can be thought of as the Holy air, or the Holy breath. We sing in our churches, "Breathe on me breath of God, fill me with life anew." Does that make better sense to you now? In Genesis 2:7 God "breathed" into Adam the breath of life and Adam became a living soul.

The only way I know to drink in a breath is to inhale. Now, I recognize, and want to say clearly, that there are many ways to experience the infilling with God's Spirit, and this miracle occurs in a great many ways. But it may help you to release your faith and receive what Jesus is doing if you drink in this pure and wonderful Living Breath by inhaling, gently, easily and deeply, through your mouth, believing that what you are being filled with is not just natural air, but the supernatural breath of God. You may notice that it is perceptibly cool and pure.

If this doesn't make sense to you don't let that bother or hinder you; go right ahead and receive anyway, in any way that is comfortable for you. The Lord is infinitely flexible.

### Receive the Holy Ghost

Now, if you are sincere and ready to receive, then close your eyes (if that will help you), put your mind on Jesus, and pray something like this:

"Lord Jesus, I thank you for saving me, healing me, delivering and comforting me. Now I want you to baptize me in your Holy Spirit, just like you did Peter, James, John, the blessed virgin Mary, Mary Magdalene, and all the others on the day of Pentecost, and like you have done for believers since that day who have asked you in faith. Fill me to overflowing with your Holy living water; I am thirsty and I have come to drink. Give me a new language with which I can pray perfect prayer and offer perfect praise. I believe you are now doing this and I am going to demonstrate my trust in you; I am going to open my mouth and thank you, not in English, but in the heavenly language you are giving me now."

Now drink fully, easily and deeply of His Spirit, several times, and let the river of thanksgiving begin to flow out of you. Speak those words, sounds and syllables out loud to Him; thank Him and tell Him how much you appreciate him, but not in English. Tell Him in the new language He is giving you! In the Name of Jesus, receive the Holy Ghost! Be free, in Jesus' Name, to pray and sing in the Spirit.

Enter in — receive the blessing and bless the Lord! And enjoy it fully. Take time to let the blessing flow. You will be filled with the Spirit many, many times as you live your life in the Spirit; but you only receive the baptism once. Enjoy it fully. Praise the Lord! Halleleuia!

# Chapter 12
# What Next?

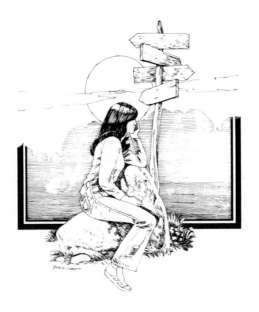

"Stand fast therefore in the liberty wherewith Christ hath made us free, and be not entangled again with the yoke of bondage."

**(Gal. 5:1)**

## Don't Be Robbed

Jesus made it plain that the devil's purpose

is to steal, kill and destroy (Jn. 10:10), and to lie to us (Jn. 8:44). Don't let him rob you of what you have received. If you let him he will rob you of your salvation, healing, deliverance, joy, Holy Spirit baptism, prayer language and every other thing with which the Lord has blessed you. Even if he can't really take them away, if he can make you think you never received them, or that they have been lost, the effect is much the same.

If you have just received the Holy Spirit baptism, the enemy has two lies prepared for you. Both are effective if you are not prepared for them.

**Lie Number One.** Very soon after you have received (sometimes immediately) — usually within 24 hours — he will come to you with a familiar lie. He will put the thought in your mind that you were just making all those words up. He sometimes tells us we were just imitating someone else. But you know it's real because Jesus promised that what you ask for is what you get (Lk 11:9-13). It is also interesting and worthwhile to note that the Lord has at times temporarily given me the same language as the one who was receiving — apparently to give the seeker confidence. On two occasions that I can remember, the seeker and I sang the same song, in the Spirit, with the same words, at the same time — a perfect duet. This is totally, unquestionably supernatural because these were songs given by the Holy Spirit which neither of us had ever heard or sung before.

When you come back at the devil's lie with the Word and refuse to doubt, he will shift to Lie Number Two.

**Lie Number Two.** This one goes about like this: "Alright, alright, OK! You really did receive the baptism in the Holy Spirit, and you really did speak in tongues — it was real. But, you will never be able to do it again — you see you have to have a heavy anointing, be on a spiritual high, be prayed for by some very spiritual person, etc. That's how it happened this first time, and you'll never be able to do it again."

Once again, the answer is the Word; when he comes against you with this one, stick the Sword of the Lord in him again and twist it. He will flee from you. Study I Cor. 14:15 carefully and you will see that it says, among other things, "I will pray in the Spirit . . ." (I will to do it — decide to do it — and I do it); " . . . I will sing in the Spirit . . ." (I will to do it — decide to do it — and I do it). In verse 32 it is plainly written "And the spirits of the prophets are subject to the prophets." In Ephesians 6:18 and Jude 20 we are exhorted to pray this way; if we were not able to comply, then these instructions would at best be silly. And the Word of God isn't silly.

The gifts and callings of God are permanent works and He neither changes His mind about them nor takes them away from us (Rom. 11:29).

Don't let anyone talk you out of what you have received from the Lord. It's real, it's yours and it's permanent.

## Don't Be Discouraged If You're Not Yet Perfect

Misunderstanding of one verse of scripture has caused a great deal of trouble for new Christians. That verse is II Corinthians 5:17 "Therefore if any man be in Christ, he is a new creature: old things are passed away; behold, all things are become new."

Now, there's nothing wrong with that verse — it's the Word of God. But there's a lot wrong with thinking it means that you are instantly made perfect — body, soul and spirit.

**But What Is A New Creature?** When you are born again you become completely new spirituallly. You have passed from death to life, darkness to light. You and the God of the Universe are now one spirit. And you will have an entirely new outlook on life. But you may still be sick; you may still have compelling negative, ungodly emotions to be dealt with; you may still have unhealthy thought habits, fears, selfish desires. Does that mean you're not really saved? Of course it doesn't! But some new believers, thinking they should be totally changed and perfected, decide that since they still have some wrong things in their lives, they really aren't born again. They are deceived into thinking they were rejected by God, that they tried to come to the Lord and failed, and they become discouraged and give up. How tragic!

God will heal your body, heal your mind, set you free from besetting sins or unhealthy emotions; but some of it takes time " . . . the inward man is renewed day by day" (II Cor. 4:16). Your mind must be renewed — washed in the Word — and your thought patterns changed (Rom. 12:2). Give Him time.

God, of course, is sovereign — He can do it all at once if He chooses. But He usually doesn't. So don't be discouraged; He will give you everything you need. But some of it may take time.

### Understand What The Baptism In the Holy Spirit Is Not

We have devoted a great many pages to what the baptism in the Holy Spirit is; now I believe it would be profitable to devote a few words to pointing out what it isn't. It should help you.

**1. It is Not Instant Maturity.** The enduement with power comes in a fraction of a millisecond; maturity takes time. In fact, so much zeal, joy, excitement and enthusiasm often come with this power that some have suggested we be locked in a cage for at least six weeks until our excitement and joy can level off. It is rather like youth. Youth is such a wonderful thing; but it seems a shame it has to be wasted on young people. Some of us would say that all that zeal, energy, resilience, etc. would be much more effective in the hands of us older and wiser people. But that doesn't seem to be God's way.

**2. It is Not Spiritual Completion.** Approximately thirty years after receiving the baptism in the Holy Spirit the Apostle Paul said that he had not yet "arrived" ("Brethren, I count not myself to have apprehended . . ." Phil. 3:13). The baptism is not the culmination of your spiritual growth and experience, it is merely a beginning, the gate through which we enter the supernatural dimension of the Christian life.

**3. It Is Not the Solution to All Spiritual Problems.** We used to think that if we could just get all the Christians baptized in the Holy Spirit all church problems would be solved. We were wrong. Anyway, Jesus never promised any such thing, and the New Testament Church had no such experience. They had lots of problems!

**4. It Is Not a Guarantee of Consistent Christian Victory.** We also used to think that once a Christian was baptized in the Spirit he couldn't possibly backslide. We were wrong again. Jesus never promised that either, and the New Testament Church had its Ananiases and Saphiras (see, for example, Acts 5:1-10; Phil. 3:17-19; I Jn. 2:19).

**5. It will Not Necessarily Make You a Better Christian than Your Neighbor who Hasn't Received It.** The baptism in the Holy Spirit will not necessarily make you a better, more effective Christian than another Christian who hasn't received it. But — and this is certain — it will definitely make you a better Christian with it than you were before you received it. The only valid comparison is the "new you" with the "old you." I know some Spirit-baptized Christians who are absolutely, unequivocally, irrefutably sorry* Christians. They make me wish they wouldn't tell anybody that they know the Lord. But — and this is so significant — they would be even sorrier Christians if they hadn't received it. It will definitely make you a better Christian than you were before. Aren't you glad?

**6. It Is Not the End of Trouble.** As a matter of fact, there will be times when it will seem like it was just the beginning. "Yea, and all that will live godly in Christ Jesus shall

---

*Outside the rural South, this adjective may need explanation. It means "of the very lowest quality, with no reasonable expectation of improvement."

suffer persecution" (II Tim. 3:12). That's a promise. Not many Christians claim it, but it is a promise nonetheless. You shall experience persecution. You won't have to seek it either — it will just happen. "Many are the afflictions of the righteous: but the Lord delivereth him out of them all" (Ps. 34:19). And Jesus said "In the world ye shall have tribulation." But, praise His holy name, He went on to remind us to "be of good cheer; I have overcome the world." And He pointed out that this happy fact should cause us to be of good cheer; He said that these things were spoken to us in order that, in Him, we might have peace (Jn. 16:33). He is truly wonderful!

Perhaps the most painful experience is in being misunderstood and rejected by the ones you really care about, the ones you want most to help, the ones you thought you could count on to trust and support you. Often it will be the ones you thought would always "act like Christians." Jesus suffered this "contradiction (hostility) of sinners against Himself" (Hebr. 12:3); He was misunderstood and deserted; He was "wounded in the house of His friends" (Zech. 13:6). He understands, He will sustain you, and He will heal you. Forgive them, then ask Him to heal you and take away the pain. He will — every time.

Yes — trouble will come to you after the baptism in the Holy Spirit; but in the trouble there should <u>never again</u> be <u>defeat</u>.

**Pray Much In The Spirit**

I have known some Spirit-baptized Christians who prayed in tongues at the time of receiving and never spoke another word in the Spirit. How very sad; they just didn't know any better. They had been taught that it was the initial evidence, the proof to the church that they had actually received, and nothing more. One Hollywood celebrity who loves the Lord received the baptism, prayed briefly in tongues, but stopped and never pursued it again because she said it frightened her. How sad. Here again is the result of that lack of knowledge. They are being robbed of this blessed provision of God, and the Kingdom is being robbed of their fully-capacitated ministry of prayer and praise.

**Do I Have to Remember the Words?** Some precious seekers are a little anxious because they think they must memorize these new words the Lord gives them. This brings us to a very important and very basic fact of life in the Spirit. Prayer, praise and messages in tongues come from your spirit, and go out your mouth. Your mind is by-passed (and, as is pointed out at the end of chapter 10, your mind is often offended by this as it has run the show up until now). This is clearly stated in I Cor. 14:14 "For if I pray in an unknown tongue, my spirit prayeth, but my understanding (mind) is unfruitful (not functioning in the prayer)." It may help make this plain to know that you cannot "think in tongues;" it simply cannot be done, except in the sense that you can remember certain words already spoken and think about them. You can pray in tongues so softly that it is virtually silent and those around you will not hear (I have done this a great deal when in church or around other people who would not understand); but one cannot "think in tongues."

There is one intriguing exception to this fact; it seems that the Lord, knowing our limitations, will sometimes put the first few words in your mind at the time of receiving. Some can even "see" the words, in the mind's eye, and spell them out. He seems to do this for some to make entering in easier. But soon after the initial experience these words leave your mind, apparently because the need is past, and the flow from your spirit becomes more and more free.

**Make It Regular.** You will want to anyway, especially at first, but see to it that you pray in your new language at least once a day. Many find that if they pray first in the Spirit, they then pray much more effectively with the understanding. There may even be significance in the order in which Paul lists the two kinds of prayer in I Cor. 14:15: "I will pray with the Spirit, and I will pray with the understanding also." Try it and see.

**Pray without Ceasing.** You will probably be praying in tongues in your sleep also — many do — because your spirit never gets tired. Actually, I think we cannot obey the command to "pray without ceasing" in I Thes. 5:17 until we are released to pray with the Spirit. Our minds and bodies eventually get tired and have to sleep. But our spirits never get tired.

**Changing Languages.** Don't be alarmed if you notice that your prayer language has changed. You will probably pray in many different languages as time goes by. One Episcopal priest who travels a great deal in public ministry has been overheard in at least nine different languages understood by someone present.

**Why Pray in the Spirit?** In addition to the fact that it seems to be a commandment (Eph. 6:18; Jude 20), the following are some of the reasons this type of prayer is so important:

**1. It edifies the one who prays or speaks** (I Cor. 14:4). The English word edify is derived from the Latin word aedificium which means "a building." To be edified simply means to be built up, to be strengthened, to be completed. Do you know any Christians who don't need this?

**2. It builds our faith** (Jude 20). Every time

you pray or speak this way it is a faith act, and you are "building yourself up on your most holy faith." Do you know anyone whose faith is too strong already?

**3. It makes possible perfect prayer and praise** (Rom. 8:26,27; I Cor. 14:14-18). This makes it possible for us to pray perfect prayer — especially when we don't know how to pray in a given situation, and to offer perfect praise. This is explained in Chapter 9.

**4. It is, for me, a pure language.** This one is strictly my idea, but I like it. It blesses me to know that I have a language with which to communicate with God that I have never used to swear or hurt someone's feelings. Those who speak that language naturally may use it for ungodly purposes, but I never have. It is, in this sense, a virgin language for me, and I think that's nice.

## Sing In The Spirit

If you can pray in tongues, you can sing in tongues. If you have never done it, a good way to enter into this blessed form of praise and worship is to get alone (if that will help you relax), close your eyes, put your mind on Jesus — visualize Him — and begin to hum. Don't hum a tune you know, just let the Spirit guide you as to when to go up, when to go down, etc. It may seem like you are "making it up" but you aren't; you are just being led by the Spirit.

As soon as the melody begins to flow, begin to put words to it with your prayer language. Then just "sing unto the Lord a new song" (Ps. 96:1; Is. 42:10, etc.); let it come from your heart and bless the Lord (you will be blessed too).

If you like to sing you will find a new dimension of joy in singing this way. If you don't sing, or if people think you don't sing well, then this is perfect for you. You will be singing a song that has never before been sung, and no one can say you didn't sing it right. Isn't that wonderful? Press on in and get blessed!

As has already been pointed out, praying and singing in the Spirit will normally be done in private — in your room, in the shower, driving in your car, or quietly and privately in church. But there will be wonderful times when an entire congregation will be inspired to sing together in the Spirit like a heavenly choir! Be sensitive to the Spirit, stay within scriptural guidelines, and enjoy this wonderful form of praise and worship.

**Use Wisdom In Sharing**

Don't be ashamed of what the Lord has done for you, and never, never deny it (Matt. 10:33; Rom. 1:16). But ask the Lord for wisdom to know how and when to share what the Lord has done for you.

If you lived among unbiased pagans then

the thing to do would be to "blaze it abroad", to tell everyone who would listen to you — to shout it from the housetops. But, more than likely, you live among biased church people and that changes things. They may not want to hear it; they may even extend to you the "left foot of Christian fellowship" and ask you to leave the church.

So what do we do? Well, that is really an individual matter, requiring individual guidance from the Lord. This may sound like dodging the issue but it's not, and it is really the only valid answer.

**Rule of Thumb.** Rules of thumb are, at best, less than perfect; but this one may help you. When you are wondering about telling people and you are not at all sure that they will be blessed by your testimony, wait until they see the change in you and ask you what has brought it about. That will be your cue to say "Well, since you asked, let me tell you what Jesus has done for me . . ."

But if the one in question is your husband or wife, don't put it off more than a very few days, whether he (she) asks about the change in you or not. If they don't give you the opening very soon, ask the Lord to prepare the way and go ahead and lay it on them. It is really unhealthy to make them feel left out of something so important in your life, even if they act like they don't want

138

to hear it.

## Don't Look Back

Get the injuries of the past, along with painful memories, healed if need be. Deal with them once and then forget them. Don't dwell on the past — you don't have a "past" anymore.

Our brother Paul expressed it perfectly: "Brethren, I count not myself to have apprehended (arrived at perfection): but this one thing I do, forgetting those things which are behind, and reaching forth unto those things which are before, I press toward the mark ..." (Phil. 3:13,14).

Learn from the past; if we don't learn from the past we are doomed to repeat it. But return one time — only — to certain experiences in the past where there is a need for confession or healing; then leave it behind and press on into what the Lord has before you. When I was a boy my father taught me how to lay off straight rows with a plow. The key is to fix your eye on a stable mark ahead — clear across the field — and keep your eye on that mark until you reach it. If you look down at the plow you will swerve to one side or the other, leaving behind you a crooked furrow; if you look back, it's hopeless. Life is like that. You cannot live effectively as a Christian if you look back and dwell on the mistakes of the past. If you want to leave a straight furrow behind the plow of your life keep your eye up ahead — on the Mark — on Jesus and His plan for your life. Forget those things which are behind; press on ahead. It's a brand new ballgame.

## Be Yourself

Each of us is unique — one of a kind. God never intended for us to be little charismatic cookies, all stamped out with the same cookie cutter. He wants you to be free to develop into the fulfilled individual He created you to become.

Each of us is unique and has a unique contribution to make. If there are two Christians in your church just alike, one of them is unnecessary. Remember that. Follow those who have set godly examples, but by all means be yourself. There's not another one like you anywhere.

# Chapter 13
# Growing In The Spirit

"As newborn babes, desire the sincere milk of the Word, that ye may grow thereby."
(I Peter 2:2)

We are all Christians under construction. Even Jesus wasn't born with it all in this sense:

in Luke 1:80 we read that ". . . the child grew, and waxed strong in spirit . . ."; and in Luke 2:52 it is written, "And Jesus increased in wisdom and stature, and in favor with God and man." He even "learned . . . obedience by the things which He suffered" (Heb. 5:8). We all must grow.

## Climbing the Mountain

As a matter of fact, if we don't continue to grow we will probably begin to slide back, losing ground and giving up hard-won victories, rather than staying at the level where we ceased to climb. A growing Christian may be compared with an automobile, driving up a long, gradual mountain grade. This automobile has a good engine, transmission, etc., and plenty of power, but no brakes. As long as it continues to climb the grade it is doing fine; the air gets purer and clearer, the view becomes more and more beautiful and of greater and greater range. Everything is fine until we begin to be satisfied with the level we have reached and decide to just stop there and settle in. We can't just stop there; for as soon as we stop climbing we begin to roll backward down the grade. Why stop anyway? It just gets better and better as we grow.

And there are some specific things we can do, and things we can learn, in order to grow spiritually as we should. In the following pages are some of the most important.

## Establish a "Quiet Time"

If you haven't already done so, establish a quiet time and be faithful to it. You cannot grow spiritually without regular prayer and study of God's Word. We <u>must</u> study the scripture "to show ourselves approved" (II Tim. 2:15), and for our minds to be renewed (Rom. 12:2); we must learn the Word of God and "hide it in our hearts" (Ps. 119:11). We must grow in faith, and faith comes primarily from feeding on the Word of God (Rom. 10:17). But it is <u>also</u> essential to spend time alone with the Lord, to pray and to listen. So pick a time which best fits you and your situation — a time which is realistic for you and when you can be <u>alone</u> without distraction. Do whatever you have to do: set the alarm clock a little earlier, take the phone off the hook, lock yourself in the bathroom or whatever it takes. But do it. Get alone with the Lord, talk to Him, give Him a chance to talk to you, and study your Bible. If you can only do it for five minutes at first, do it; but most people need more than that. Start where you are, take it slow and easy, and let the Lord lead you.

Generally speaking, it seems better to do this early in the morning. It gets us off to a good start on the day, and the scriptures seem to indicate it. Jesus taught us to pray "Give us this day," not "Give us the day that just ended" (Matt. 6:11). Abraham had a regular place to seek the Lord, and seems to have gone there early in the morning (Gen. 19:27). Jesus was an early riser; but then He sometimes prayed all night. I am an early riser and the only quality time I can have with the Lord is early in the morning. David Wilkerson gets his best time of prayer and Bible reading after midnight; I'm just not wired that way — I fade out late at night.

Don't be legalistic about it — it's not so important when you do it, as it is that you do it — but if you can manage it for the beginning of your day it will bless you.

**And Stick With It.** When you miss a day you will notice the difference — and it won't be good. If you miss two days your family and friends will probably notice the difference. Miss three days and everybody will notice. Stick with it (A disciple is one who is disciplined) — you need it and the Lord desires it. You and He will both be blessed.

### Stay in Fellowship

Find fellowship with like-minded believers and stay close. We need one another. Don't try to be a spiritual Lone Ranger — that's dangerous and unscriptural. There may be times when the Lord will call you apart to spend a period of time just with Him; but, generally speaking, it is extremely important to find fellowship and stay in it. We bless one another, strengthen one another, balance one another and protect one another. Besides this, it is clearly the scriptural pattern and God's intention that each of us find his or her place in the Body of Christ and fit into it.

**A Knotty Problem At Times.** Let me warn you, in case you haven't already found out, that this may not be simple. It is a sensitive matter and there are many pitfalls. Many churches do not teach, or even accept as valid, what you are entering into; in such a spiritual environment you will find it hard to grow — or even to be comfortable. You may be part of such a church. If the Lord impresses upon you that you are to stay there and be a light to them then you must do so. But if you must be part of a church that doesn't declare and minister the full gospel, find a Bible study or prayer group which does. If you want to be in on the move of God, you must go where God is moving; and He only moves where He is free to. Don't leave your church unless you are sure that you are being directed to by the Lord; but by the same token it is a mistake to stay in a "dead" church if the Lord has given you liberty to go. In such a situation what generally happens is that the fire will go out in you, rather than your fire's spreading through the church. Dwight L. Moody, perhaps the greatest evangelist of modern times, was accused of urging the newly-saved people in his meetings to "leave their churches." He really didn't do that and felt that it would be wrong; but he said that neither could he, in good conscience recommend "putting live chicks under a dead hen."

**Love is the Key.** If you are going to stay, and be a spark of revival in your church, it can only be accomplished through loving them. Let Jesus shine brightly and quietly through you. Love them — even when they persecute you and say hateful things about you (and, incidentally, they probably will). Love — the love of God — is an irresistable force, the ultimate weapon. Turn it loose on them. Blow them away with agape! Some of them, at least, will want to know what you have.

**A Word of Caution.** Some churches, Bible studies and prayer groups are to be avoided, especially at first. It is regrettable, but some have been led off into error and will take you with them. Some groups have started off filled with pure love and zeal for the Lord, His Word and His Kingdom, bubbling over with the Spirit, but then were deceived and led into error by a false teaching, overemphasis of a valid teaching, or by a persuasive leader. Be very careful. There are pitfalls along the way, and some of them will be attractive. Avoid the following, especially at first:

1. Learning from only one teacher (especially one who says everybody else is wrong). There is safety in a multitude of counsellors (Prov. 11:14).

2. A group that follows only one man's teachings, or the teachings of only one group or "family" of teachers.

3. A group that would isolate you from all other fellowship. If the leader puts you in fear that if you should leave you will be in danger, then there is only one thing to do. Leave (Rom. 8:15; II Tim. 1:7).

4. A group (or teacher) given to a heavy emphasis on emotional experiences, "feelings", and prophetic utterance, and which does not base all action on, and devote most of its time to, study of the scriptures themselves. Christians in such groups usually stop growing, lose their joy, become confused, fearful and excessively devoted to the leader. If you are hearing more "prophecy" than you are hearing solid teaching of the Word, something is wrong. The "prophet" may become the focal point rather than Jesus.

5. Exclusivism — standards of commitment and performance which will cause "ordinary" or struggling Christians to be looked down upon as inferior, or as "losers", not overcomers "like our group". Such groups usually

end up with a relatively small number of completely dedicated, strong believers; but they leave many weak and struggling believers broken and bleeding along the roadside, discouraged and condemned.

6. Groups which have closed meetings. I know of no scriptural precedent for this, other than the short period immediately after the crucifixion when the disciples had themselves locked in for fear. Jesus said "What I tell you in darkness, that speak ye in light; and what ye hear in the ear, that preach ye upon the housetops" (Matt. 10:27).

7. Groups which are strongly committed to a particular doctrine. People in such groups will often talk more about the doctrine than about Jesus. They may go out and "witness" on the streets about their doctrine — tracts and all. Another earmark of such groups is that they tend to be argumentative, and if you question their doctrine they usually become angry.

8. Legalism. God is not legalistic. Jesus fought religious legalism, teaching that what really matters is not so much what we do or how we do it as what is in our hearts, "The letter killeth, but the spirit giveth life" (II Cor. 3:6). Beware of stern teaching of absolutes. Legalism is an attitude. It crushes and condemns. Flee from it.

Now, don't be afraid; go on and find fellowship. Be careful as you seek it, but seek it. And when you find it, enter in.

## Be Baptized in Water

If you have never been validly baptized in water you need to be. Water baptism is inseparably linked in the scriptures with salvation (Matt. 28:18-20; Mk. 16:15-18; Acts 2:38; Acts 8:12; Acts 9:17,18; etc.). It is much more than a symbol or an act of obedience (although it is both of these things also). Study Romans 6:1-13, Gal. 3:26-29 and Col. 2:8-12; seek the Lord about this and then decide for yourself two things:

1. What is valid water baptism?
2. Have I received it?

If you decide, after study and prayer that you have never been validly baptized in water then you need to receive this blessing as soon as possible.

**Again, A Word of Caution.** Don't let anyone convince you that you are not validly baptized in water unless certain words are spoken over you. This is legalism at best; and it can be something much worse. There are pharisees out there who will put you in bondage over this if you let them. Don't allow it (Gal. 5:1).

## I Hate to Sound Negative, But . . .

All this about persecution, trouble and cautions about pitfalls to be avoided may seem negative. I pray that it isn't. And if I had put it at the beginning you probably would not have read the rest of the book. But these things are real. They are there in the road before you, and someone needs to warn you (Prov. 2:10,11). People will all, sooner or later, disappoint you — count on it. That, in a sense, is "the bad news". (Knowing this, you won't be knocked off the track when it happens.) "The good news" is that Jesus never will. <u>Keep your eyes on Him — not on people</u>, no matter how appealing or persuasive they may be.

### Learn to Share the Good News

One reason the church grew so rapidly during its first years was that one Jewish lady, who was redeemed, forgiven, free and excited about it, ran next door and told her neighbors. Then <u>they</u> received the Lord, experienced this wonderful reality and ran to tell <u>their</u> neighbors. And so it went. They multiplied geometrically — the gospel spread like wildfire! And they didn't go through a period of formal training before they told their neighbors — they had simply found something wonderful and wanted to share it. It was that simple, and so far we don't seem to be improving on their results.

But there <u>are</u> some things we can learn about effectively sharing the Good News and helping others find this relationship that we have found with Jesus. Learn the scriptures which apply to salvation. There are a great many, but pick out those with which you can work best and learn them (until you have them memorized, write them down inside your Bible). For many this will be "the Roman Road to salvation" scriptures: Rom. 3:23; Rom. 6:23; Rom. 5:8 and Rom 10:8-13. As time goes by you will settle on those which are most satisfactory to you, but start somewhere. Start now.

Ask the Lord every day to give you at least one person to talk to about the Lord and what He has done in your life. And when you speak with them, do it in your own words; keep it simple, keep it personal, and never argue (we are witnesses — not lawyers). It is also good to select a salvation tract that is suitable for your purposes and carry a few with you at all times so that you can leave the person with something he can retain — something with scripture references in it. Your greatest joy will come in sharing with others the wonderful Good News of Jesus and seeing them born into His Kingdom.

## Understand the Gifts of the Spirit and Ministries in the Church

The matter of spiritual gifts and ministries in the church is a separate subject and one too vast for full treatment in this book. But a basic knowledge of gifts, ministries and how they relate to one another is essential in order to understand what you are experiencing, and to begin to grow and function in the Spirit as we should.

**Gifts Versus Ministries.** The first thing necessary to understand is the difference between gifts and ministries. A ministry is a function, job or office within the church — a part of the overall life and operation of the local church and, ultimately, the Body of Christ. There are many ministries, virtually an unlimited number, from apostle, prophet, evangelist, pastor and teacher to administration, giving, governing, healing, speaking messages in tongues, interpreting tongues, driving a bus or van, intercessory prayer, maintenance, calling and visiting the lonely, etc.

The supernatural gifts of the Spirit, on the other hand, are nine spiritual weapons or tools the Lord releases in our lives so that we can fulfill the ministry(ies) to which He has called us. The basic Bible teaching on gifts and ministries is found in I Cor. 12 where the first part of the chapter (verses 1-11) deals with gifts, and the latter part (verses 27-31) deals with ministries in the church.

**The Nine Supernatural Gifts of the Spirit.** There are many functions in the Church referred to in the New Testament as "gifts" (Rom. 12:6-8; I Cor. 12:8-10; Eph. 4:11) however, the nine listed in I Cor. 12:8-10 are different from all the others in one very significant respect — they are supernatural. These nine gifts are sovereign, supernatural operations of the Spirit of God and He decides when, and through whom, they will be manifested. "But all these worketh that one and the selfsame Spirit, dividing to every man severally as He will" (I Cor. 12:11).

No one "has" any of these gifts in the sense that they possess title deed to them and can operate them whenever they wish; rather, all believers may at one time or another be used as vessels by the Holy Spirit to manifest one or more of these gifts. Let me use a familiar illustration to explain. If I want to bless my daughter with a gift of some beautiful roses — just because I love her and want to encourage her — I select a florist, pay for the roses and decide when they are to be delivered. At this point a delivery boy is selected for the privilege of delivering the roses to her. He puts them in his van, drives to her house, knocks at the door and has the joy of handing her this unexpected gift and seeing her blessed. Then he goes back to the flower shop — his part in all this is finished. Whose gift is it? My daughter's. Was it his? No! Does he "have the gift of roses"? Of course not! I paid for them, decided where and when they would be delivered, and the gift belongs to my daughter. He was only the delivery boy — it's a nice job, delivering blessings to people, but he was only the delivery boy. And, next time, a different delivery boy may be selected.

Don't you see how it works? These gifts are from the Lord (He has paid for them), to His children, for the purpose of blessing them, encouraging them and meeting their needs. And He decides which of us will be the "delivery boy" (that's really all we are), selecting different ones at different times (". . . dividing to every man severally as He will").

And notice that in I Cor. 12:6,7, speaking of these gifts, the Bible says "And there are diversities of operations, but it is the same God which worketh all in all. But the manifestation of the Spirit is given to every man (woman or child) to profit withal (for the common good)." These nine manifestations, then, may all occur at one time or another in the lives of each believer. Briefly they are:

1. **Word of Wisdom.** This is not the "gift of wisdom"; there is no such thing. It is the gift of the word of wisdom; this is a tiny portion of the wisdom of God, imparted momentarily so that we can say just the right thing at just the right time (Jn. 8:1-7). This will often answer a question in the other person's mind when the question hasn't even been spoken.

2. **The Word of Knowledge.** again, this is not "the gift of knowledge", but the gift of the word of knowledge. This is the occasional im-

parting of a tiny fragment of the total knowledge of God for use in a specific situation. This knowledge, obviously supernatural, is often used by the Lord to convict (Jn. 4:16-19) or to help others to release faith to receive a healing or some other blessing from God.

**3. Faith.** This is a momentary release of extraordinary faith within the believer to make possible extraordinary acts. No one just walks around with this kind of faith — it's the kind Peter needed to walk on the water (Matt. 14:29).

**4. Gifts of Healing.** Notice that the Bible pluralizes this one: it is "gifts", not "gift". This is the occasional, momentary release of the healing power of God to meet a specific need. I believe that each such healing is one gift of healing — a gift from a loving Heavenly Father to someone in need (Acts 3:1-16).

**5. Working of Miracles.** This is simply what the name implies: the performing of miraculous acts by the power of the Holy Spirit. An example is the casting out of evil spirits (Acts 8:6,7).

**6. Prophecy.** Prophecy is speaking forth the words of God, to the church assembled (or to individuals), in a language understood by the hearers (Acts 21:11). There may or may not be foretelling of the future involved; prophecy is "forth-telling," not necessarily "foretelling".

The gift of prophecy is for the purpose of edifying, exhorting and comforting God's people (I Cor. 14:3).

7. **Discerning of Spirits.** Here again, because so many may not read this carefully, I must point out what it isn't. This is not "the gift of discernment" for there is no such gift in the Bible. This is discerning of spirits, and it is the momentary, occasional ability to discern the presence and nature of spirits. The most obvious application is the discerning of evil spirits or demon spirits (Acts 16:16-19). It can also involve discerning angelic spirits or the spirit of a man (Acts 8:20,21), as well as (perhaps) discerning the spirit of a meeting or service.

8. **Tongues.** This is the speaking forth, to the church assembled (occasionally also to an individual), a prophetic message in a language unknown to the one speaking, and, ordinarily, unknown to the hearers. It must then be interpreted to the hearers in a language they understand.

9. **Interpretation of Tongues.** This is the speaking forth, in a language understood by the hearers, the interpretation or meaning of a message previously spoken in tongues. It is not a word-for-word translation of the message (although it can be), but an interpretation of its meaning. That is why there can be a short message in tongues with a long interpretation,

or vice-versa. Tongues, plus interpretation, are the equivalent of prophecy.

**It is Entirely Up To You.** Manifestation of the supernatural gifts of the Spirit is just like everything else the Lord does in our lives: it is entirely voluntary. He will never force us to be vessels for His gifts, but we will be blessed (and so will He) when we trust Him enough to say "yes" to Him and are used in this way.

## Discover Your Ministry

I believe that the Lord has a ministry for every believer — at least one (Rom. 12:4-8; I Cor. 12:14-30; Eph. 4:11,12). When each of us learns this, discovers what his own function is and then begins to perform it, the Body of Christ will truly begin to function as Jesus intended. Seek from the Lord the knowledge of what He is calling you to do and He will reveal it. It may take a while, but you will know. Then earnestly desire "the best gifts" and He will release them in your life. He will enable you — the Lord will release in you the ability to do what He wants you to do (I Tim. 1:12).

**But What Are the "Best" Gifts?** This statement in I Cor. 12:31 has been misunderstood and misrepresented by so many! It cannot mean that some gifts are better than others, or that some are desirable and others undesirable. It just can't mean that, because everything God does is perfect. To suggest that some of His creations are fine, but that others are not so fine is absurd, if not blasphemous. Well, if it doesn't mean that some gifts are better than others, just what does it mean? I believe the "best" gifts are those which best fulfill the ministry to which you have been called — those which best fulfill God's purposes in your life. Open your life to them — covet them earnestly — and expect that the Lord will select and release within your life the ones you need. He doesn't make mistakes.

And remember, He may have more than one ministry for you — He often does (I Tim. 2:7). In due time He will reveal them.

**A Word of Caution Here Also.** When God calls you to a ministry (healing, teaching, intercessory prayer, administration, helps, etc.) He will do three essential things:

1. He will prepare you. This may take time (Gal. 1:15-18) and can be painful; remember the fire (Matt. 3:11; Lk. 3:16).

2. He will enable you. If you feel you are not able to do the work, remember that He will make you able (I Tim. 1:12).

3. He will provide the opportunity to perform it — He will open the doors of a ministry to you. Of course if you want to you can force a door of ministry open and rush on in; but you will wish you hadn't, for you will probably find yourself in there alone (I Cor 16:7-9; II Cor.

2:12).

So seek to know, seek to grow, and make yourself available to the Lord. But try not to be in a hurry. God's timing is always perfect.

## Learn to Use Your Spiritual Authority

Jesus established His Church, endowed it with supernatural gifts and ministries, armed it with spiritual weapons (II Cor. 10:4; Eph. 6:14-18) and gave it complete power and authority over all the works and power of the kingdom of darkness (Lk. 10:19). Then, in case there was any doubt as to the outcome, He promised complete victory (Matt. 16:18). He made it plain that He was sending the Church as a mighty, irresistable army in the attack against the forces of darkness who would be cowering behind the gates of hell, hoping the gates would protect them. But Jesus had it all set up for us, and promised that as we aggressively batter the gates down they "shall not prevail" against us. If we will take the weapons of our warfare and attack, victory is assured.

And yet for centuries the church has been sitting around, wringing its hands in fear, asking Jesus to protect it from the gates!

Hey — that makes no sense at all! It's time we learned to put on our spiritual armor, pick up our spiritual weapons, and start pulling down those unhealthy, ungodly strongholds in our lives and in the lives of others. Learn to use your authority as a believer against temptations, wrong thoughts, fears, sickness, compulsions and other unhealthy emotions. Use it against all the works of the devil that come against you, your family, your church or those to whom you minister. In the name of Jesus bind them, and command them to cease. Break their power in Jesus' name and watch them crumble and flee! It will change your life; and we should have been doing it all along, for what we have struggled against is not flesh and blood, but the works of the spirits of darkness (Eph. 6:10-12). And we have had authority over them all along, whether we realized it or not.

## Learn to Recognize, and Deal With, the Fleshly Nature

Again, there is not enough space in a book of this scope to fully explain and discuss the fleshly nature and its on-going struggle against the spiritual nature developing within us. But it needs to be introduced here, and then you can make a separate study.

What the Bible means when speaking of "the flesh" (in its struggle against the Spirit) is not the physical body, but the sinful nature (Gal. 5:17). In writing the New Testament (which was originally written in Greek), the Greek word which was used for the physical body is "soma"; but the Greek word used for "the flesh" is a completely different word, "sarx". So, you see, they are not the same. Read Galatians 5:17-25 and Romans 7:14-25 and you see the nature of the struggle. Then read Romans 6 and you see that there is a way to deal with the sinful, fleshly nature — a way to victory over "self." And then read a wonderful promise in Galatians 5:16 and know that as we grow, and learn to walk in the Spirit, we will become more and more victorious — more and more free. It is apparently a battle that goes on, a battle with ourselves, and it is often painful; but victory belongs to us. Praise the Lord!

### Stay Filled

D. L. Moody, a Spirit-baptized, mighty man of God, often spoke of the need to "get his cup filled." When asked why this should be necessary when he had been filled with the Spirit many years before, he replied, "It leaks." When the Syrophonecian woman touched the garment of Jesus and received her healing He felt the power go out of Himself — felt Himself being emptied (Mk. 5:30; Lk. 6:19).

You will find that when you minister to others in the Spirit, pray for them or counsel with them, often you will afterward feel empty and dry; at times this emptiness will be intense. But all you have to do is ask Jesus to fill

161

you afresh and He will. We probably should do this at least every day — His supply is unlimited (John 7:37,38) and our need is continuous.

In Acts 4:31 we read that those early believers, rejoicing over the release of Peter and John, were filled with the Holy Ghost. What? Weren't Peter, John and the rest all baptized and filled with the Spirit already? Of course they were — many days before, at Pentecost. But the Lord filled them, afresh and anew, until the place where they were praying shook! And what was the result? Notice this now — "They spake the Word of God with boldness."

Ask the Lord to fill you up — everytime you get empty — and you will speak the Word of God with boldness too.

## And Finally

Jesus said "But ye shall receive power, after that the Holy Ghost is come upon you: and ye shall be witnesses unto me . . ." He has given you new life in the Spirit; He has given you the power you need to live in victory. Now go and live it — live it before a sick and dying world, before the discouraged and hopeless around you. Let your light shine, let it bring hope to them and be a guiding beacon to bring them to the Source of that light. Go into your home, into your neighborhood, into your community, your state, even to the uttermost parts of the Earth — wherever He sends you.

Yes, come and live! Then go and be a witness unto Him. Go share this life with others who need it, and He will go with you, confirming the Word with signs and wonders. He will go with you all the way — even to the end of the world. That's His promise, and with Him at your side you can't fail.

# Index

166